Faith Beyond Faith Healing

Finding Hope After Shattered Dreams

Kimberly Winston

PARACLETE PRESS
BREWSTER, MASSACHUSETTS

Unless otherwise designated, Scripture quotations are taken from the King James Version of the Bible.

Scripture excerpts marked (NAB) in this work are taken from the *New American Bible with Revised New Testament and Revised Psalms* © 1991, 1986, 1970 Confraternity of Christian Doctrine, Washington, D.C. Used with permission. All rights reserved. No part of the *New American Bible* may be reproduced in any form without permission in writing from the copyright owner.

Scripture quotations marked (NIV) are taken from the HOLY BIBLE, NEW INTERNATIONAL VERSION. NIV. Copyright 1973, 1978, 1984 by International Bible Society. Used by permission of Zondervan Publishing House. All rights reserved.

Library of Congress Cataloging-in-Publication Data

Winston, Kimberly, 1964–
    Faith beyond faith healing : finding hope after shattered dreams / Kimberly Winston.
        p. cm.
Includes bibliographical references (p. 146).
        ISBN 1-55725-299-8
        1. Spiritual healing. 2. Sick—Religious life—Case studies.
3. Terminally ill—Religious life—Case studies. I. Title.
        BT732.5 .W58 2002
        234'.131—dc21   2001006923

10 9 8 7 6 5 4 3 2 1

© 2002 by Kimberly Winston

ISBN: 1-55725-299-8

Published by Paraclete Press
Brewster, Massachusetts
www.paracletepress.com

Printed in the United States of America.

CONTENTS

PREFACE

> **Faith healing**—recourse to divine power to cure mental or physical disabilities, either in conjunction with orthodox medical care or in place of it.
>
> *Merriam-Webster's Encyclopedia of World Religions*

For as long as people have believed in the divine, so have they believed in divine intervention in their earthly existence. And as long as people have believed in God's interest in their personal affairs, so have they believed in faith healing.

Faith healing—the belief that God can and does cure illness and disease—spans virtually every religious culture and comes in almost as many forms. For the purposes of this book, we will concern ourselves only with faith healing expressed in the larger Judeo-Christian realm, both mainstream and nontraditional. For people of this background, faith healing can be as simple as the laying on of hands, or as complicated as a journey halfway around the world to imbibe some purported healing water or to touch some icon revered as having restorative powers. Whatever form it takes, faith healing has a long and varied history.

In the best examples of faith healing, the sick person is "cured." We have all heard tales of the blind man who suddenly sees, the lame person who suddenly walks, and the terminally ill person who goes into remission. Those cases, impossible to document to the satisfaction of both science and religion as true "acts of God," are nonetheless wonderful for the hope and inspiration they offer all believers, both the sick and the whole.

But what happens when a person of faith who is stricken seriously ill seeks some form of faith healing, and does not receive the cure he or she so desperately sought? Do they feel forgotten, abandoned, even abused by God? Or, do they find some kind of meaning in their suffering and, in the process, redefine their own beliefs in and expectations of the divine? This book is not about the very fortunate people who believe God healed them when they asked him to, but about those who either never got the healing they prayed for, or are still waiting for an answer to their prayers. How do they keep their faith in the seeming emptiness of God's silence? How do they come to terms with a God who may not answer their prayers in the way they hoped?

This book started as a story I wrote for the *Dallas Morning News's* religion section in February 2000. When I pitched the story to my editor, Diane Connolly, I thought I would wind up writing about angry, discouraged people who had turned their backs on God in disappointment over his seeming inability or unwillingness to help them in their time of greatest need. But the stories I ultimately heard surprised me. With only one or two exceptions, everyone I spoke with said that while they continued to confront their own illnesses, and in some cases their own impending deaths, they had found a faith in God that was deeper and more meaningful than the faith they had before they became ill. And, virtually everyone had come to rethink their idea of what faith healing includes, moving from the belief that it could mean only a cure for their physical condition, to believing it could mean patching up relationships, overcoming addictions, and, most important, finding some peace.

The purpose of this book is not to dissuade anyone from believing in faith healing in any of its forms, from intercessory prayer to televangelism. Nor is it to "prove" that any instance of faith healing is real. And it isn't to suggest that the experiences of the persons described here are representative of all members of a single faith. It is simply to provide a brief history of faith healing and to tell the stories of a handful of people pacing the lonely path of suffering. Somehow, they found the strength and ability to form an abiding—and ultimately healing—faith on their own.

Kimberly Winston

ACKNOWLEDGMENTS

I would like to thank everyone I interviewed for this book for their time, their thoughtfulness, their frankness, and especially their patience dealing with a journalist working on her first book. I would especially like to extend a heartfelt thank you to the subjects of this book and their survivors for their candor and honesty, especially Vicki Crenshaw, Pati Boyle, Chris Potter, Marie Duncan, Robert and Linda Shepherd, and Father Richard Bain. I would also like to thank the many friends and peers who administered much-needed advice or read various drafts—Ari Goldman, Samuel Freedman, Lynn Garrett, Phyllis Tickle, Randall Balmer, Jeff Sheler, and, most especially, Diane Connolly. And none of this would have been possible without the thoughtfulness and attention of my editor, Lil Copan, and my publisher, Lillian Miao. I'd also like to say thank you to my family, who put up with all my nonsense during the writing of this book—my sons Shawn and Chris, husband Terry, and my mom and dad, Diann and Randall Wilson. Thank you, everyone.

Kimberly Winston

Remember, God Was There Before You

The Story of Mary Elizabeth Turk

As she stands in a central Texas cemetery before a gray granite marker, the wind sweeps across the softly rising hills and brings the bitter sting of cold rain into Vicki Crenshaw's face.

Bending away from the rain, Vicki bustles about the grave, clearing the ruined flowers that mark her last visit and replacing them with the store-bought crispness of silk sunflowers. Their yellow blooms scream for attention across the starkness of the cemetery. The carved gray stone at her feet bears two hearts entwined with a dove. Beneath the family name of Turk is engraved the word "Kismet." Fate. Hands in her coat pockets against the cold, Vicki says only, "Love you, Mom," pivoting on one foot before tears can fall.

Later, after leaving the soggy cemetery behind, Vicki sips tea in the nearby small, white clapboard house that was her mother's home before she died. She turns her watery eyes to a picture of her mother that she has placed on the table. "I have three children, but my mother has probably been the most central figure in my life," she says. "She inspired me with her faith. On the one hand, you can see the erroneous horror of what happened to her, but on the other hand, you see someone who was so centered and so faith-based, she changed my life."

After eight years, Vicki still struggles to understand how fate played with her and her mother—remembered here in granite as Mary Elizabeth—through a Christian televangelist named Robert Tilton.

Mary Elizabeth Turk was born Mary Elizabeth Southern on June 29, 1924, in the small farming community of Coppell, Texas. Its corn fields are now surrounded by the rushing freeways and monotonous strip malls of modern Dallas. When Mary Elizabeth was four, her mother and father separated, and her mother packed up her seven children—an eighth was on the way—and returned to Mineral Wells, her hometown about eighty miles to the west.

Born into a Christian family, Mary Elizabeth in her adulthood became what is known as a full-gospel Pentecostal. She believed in "gifts of the Spirit," which Pentecostals hold as the divinely inspired practices of speaking in tongues, prophesying, and healing. For Mary Elizabeth, such "signs and wonders" were to be expected—indeed, they were promised, her Pentecostal faith taught her, by God in the Bible.

Pentecostalism is as old as the New Testament. In the Acts of the Apostles, the first Pentecost was celebrated by Jesus' followers, gathered together in his name from the four corners of what was then the known world. As they prayed, they were surrounded by a great rush of wind that they recognized as the Holy Spirit moving among them. Tongues "as of fire" circled their heads, and they found they were able to understand each others' native languages. The first Pentecost was thought to presage the coming of the

Last Days and the Apocalypse, something modern Pentecostals continue to look for as imminent.

Not long before Mary Elizabeth's birth, Pentecostalism experienced its biggest revival in 2,000 years. On April 9, 1906, at a gathering of largely African-American servants and laborers on Azusa Street in Los Angeles, California, the "fire from heaven" seemed to descend a second time. In what came to be known as the Azusa Street Revival, worshippers in the small, wooden storefront church broke into a kind of ecstasy, speaking in tongues, performing healings, receiving prophecy, dancing and singing in the aisles. Just as they had at the first Pentecost, these signs and wonders were again thought to herald the Second Coming of Christ. The Azusa Street revival lasted more than a year, and news of its "fire" soon spread across the country. The news spread, largely through word of mouth, itinerant ministers, and newspaper accounts in religious publications; and small Pentecostal churches appeared in its wake, especially in the rural South.

When Mary Elizabeth was growing up in the late 1920s and early 1930s, she attended Mineral Wells's Church of Christ, a fundamentalist Christian congregation that would most likely have been affected, at least slightly, by the new "fire." At the very least, her congregation, like so many others, took its Bible literally. The Bible said God could heal, so Mary Elizabeth believed God could heal. She believed he took interest in the individual lives of his children. She believed in miracles.

And why shouldn't she? Mineral Wells was a town built on healing miracles. When Judge James A. Lynch settled there in 1877, he dug a well for drinking water that local people believed cured their sicknesses. By 1880, there were three "healing" wells dug in Mineral Wells, and the town's lore holds that a mentally deranged woman came and drank from the well every day. When she and others pronounced herself cured, the reputation of Mineral Wells's healing water spread throughout Texas. Mary Elizabeth grew up on these stories.

In 1942, Mary Elizabeth married Robert R. Turk, an Air Force man. Everywhere they were posted, in Wyoming, California, Texas, and Germany, her leather-bound Bible went with her and she read from it every day. And although she and her family regularly worshipped in the rather generic chapels found on military bases, Mary Elizabeth instilled her fundamentalist Christian beliefs in her seven children—four boys and three girls.

Robert Turk retired in 1971, and several years later the couple moved back to Mineral Wells and built a tiny cabin on family land. Not long after, Robert, a smoker, fell ill with emphysema and a series of heart ailments. He died in 1990, his last days filled with pain, doctors, and more pain.

Mary Elizabeth and her children buried Robert Turk in Sturdevant Cemetery, a somewhat forlorn, fenced-in patch of ground a couple of miles from downtown Mineral Wells. Mary Elizabeth returned to her small house, alone for the first time in her life. She couldn't sleep, and she began watching a lot of television. One of the programs she watched was called "Success-N-Life." It featured a handsome, silver-haired minister named Robert Tilton.

Robert Tilton rolled into Dallas, Texas, in the spring of 1976, his wife and two children in tow. He was wrapping up eighteen months of holding tent-style revivals across the South. With the help of a few Dallas friends and followers, he started the Word of Faith Church in a rented YMCA hall. At the first service in March 1976, there were seven people, including the new minister and his wife. Like many Pentecostal ministers, he had no formal Bible or seminary training, but relied on his own interpretation of Scripture and personal charisma to attract followers.

By 1990, Tilton's Word of Faith Church had 8,000 members packed into its newly constructed facility off Interstate 35 in Farmers Branch, a suburb of the Dallas metroplex that hadn't seen a tractor in decades. Wearing $2,000 suits, driving a Mercedes and a Jaguar, and resting his head in a $4.5 million mansion, Tilton seemed to be the personification of what he preached: that God wants his children to be happy, healthy, and, most important, prosperous. All he asks in return, Tilton taught, is that you believe—believe without question.

Tilton's theology owed a debt to Asa A. Allen, another Dallas-based evangelist whose national radio broadcasts were enormously popular in the 1950s and 1960s. On his show and in tent revivals, Allen was known to hawk "prayer cloths," bits of fabric he claimed were anointed with "Miracle Oil." During a revival in 1962 in Philadelphia, he announced that God "had given him a new anointing and a new power to lay hands on the believers who gave $100 . . . and bestow upon each of them POWER TO GET WEALTH."[1] Allen's teaching, which came to be known as the "prosperity gospel," still has a large following today, especially in the ministries of Kenneth Hagin, Kenneth Copeland, John Avanzini, and T.D. Jakes. Robert Tilton had a taste for it, too.

Like Allen, Tilton owed much of his popularity and prosperity to his broadcast audience. His "Success-N-Life" television show first aired in 1984 on six Christian television stations, and by 1990 it had spread to almost 200 stations around the world. Tilton's crinkly eyes and lacquered silver mane made daily appearances in the living rooms of more than a million households in the United States alone.

In the mid-1980s, about ten years after opening the doors to his Word of Faith Church, Robert Tilton turned to direct mail appeals for money. Up to then, he had relied mostly on call-in donations during his television show. In the late 1980s, he enlisted the services of two direct mail companies in Tulsa, Oklahoma, more than 300 miles from his church and television studio in Dallas. By 1990, Tilton's direct mail list numbered 880,000 addresses. When, that same year, *USA Today* estimated his ministry's assets at $25 million, he famously sniffed that the estimate was too low. Scott Baradell, a reporter for the *Dallas Observer*, wrote in 1992 that according to a three-week financial report he had seen, Tilton was likely pulling in $120 million per year.

About the time Robert Tilton scorned the report of his worth in *USA Today*, Mary Elizabeth began to experience pain. Her stomach and lower back hurt, sometimes terribly, and she started losing sleep. For a while, she hid her illness from her now grown children, including her three sons and a daughter who lived near her in Mineral Wells. But one thing she was sure of after watching her husband's lingering death: There would be no doctors for her. The only thing that brought relief was watching that nice young Reverend Tilton on the television in the kitchen. She especially liked to watch him late at night, when the pain was so bad it stole her sleep.

On the television, she heard Tilton describe the numerous healings he claimed were experienced by people—especially those who sent him money. When people sent him money, he said, it was a show of their faith in God's blessings. And God's blessings were not only something Mary Elizabeth devoutly believed in, but something she also needed badly. One day, she called the number at the bottom of her television screen. The phone rang in Tulsa. A "prayer minister" listened as Mary Elizabeth described her pain. He took her name and address and added it to Robert Tilton's databank.

Within weeks, the mail appeals began. In the first envelope, Mary Elizabeth received a poster of Tilton with his eyes closed and his hands clasped in prayer. It came with instructions to place her hand over his photograph every day and pray. He would be praying for her, too, the enclosed letter said. The instructions suggested she tape the poster to her refrigerator. They also suggested that if she didn't send Tilton some cash, his prayers for her wouldn't work.

First, Mary Elizabeth sent three dollars. Then the pink envelopes came faster and faster, each bearing an urgent plea in handwritten words, as though Tilton had composed the letters himself, just for Mary Elizabeth. Most of the mailings came with at least one black-and-white photocopy of Tilton's handsome face, usually scrunched up as if in torment from the pain in other people's lives. One contained a small, supposedly anointed prayer cloth and the request that she stash it beneath her pillow. She did. Another contained two pennies and promised that if she sent them back multiplied many times over in a personal check, he would deposit them in his "New Testament Treasury Chest" and pray over them—and her—every day. Mary Elizabeth Turk sent Robert Tilton a check for $1,000.

Meanwhile, Mary Elizabeth's pain became so bad she could no longer hide it from her family. The brown hair she usually kept waved and fluffed about her face was now limp and mussed. Her once-full face became sunken and thin. Her eyes, usually framed in a lattice of smile lines, now peered out from a deep field of wrinkles. Once a plumpish matron, she lost weight. All of her children became concerned. From Dallas, Vicki pleaded with her mother to go to a doctor. She drove to Mineral Wells frequently to make her case in person to her mother. Once, Vicki even got down on her hands and knees and begged her mother. But each time, Mary Elizabeth refused. Finally, when her mother's illness became debilitating, Vicki gave up her job as a student adviser at Dallas's Southern Methodist University and moved in with her mother, sleeping in the small bedroom just across the narrow hall from her mother's.

Not long after moving in with her mother, Vicki was tidying up when she came across a stack of Tilton's pink envelopes. She saw the pictures, the pleas for money, the prayer cloth, the pennies. It was the first time she had ever heard of Robert Tilton.

She confronted her mother. "Is this what has been influencing you?" she asked her mother, a pile of what she called "that crap" in her hands. Mary Elizabeth said it was. She described how she had sent Rev. Tilton some money, but explained that it was not a waste, as Vicki thought, but "a show of faith." In the next weeks, the two women did battle. Vicki usually ended up pulling out this Bible Scripture or that, usually about false prophets. But her mother always pulled out another one, usually about abiding faith. Vicki, also a life-long Christian, shared her mother's belief in God's goodness and his blessings. But she also believed that her mother, who had never held a job and always lived a rather sheltered life on military bases, knew very little of the world. "She actually had the idea that he was reading her mail personally," Vicki says. "Mother thought he was personally in touch with her all this time." Vicki tried showing her mother that Tilton's signatures at the bottom of his letters were mass-produced, by licking her finger and running it over the ink to smear it. But her mother had no idea what computers were capable of. She remained unconvinced. And, she continued to refuse to see a doctor. "She felt that it would be a breach of faith," Vicki explains. "Robert Tilton managed to convince her that if she remained steadfast, this would be an extreme show of faith; and the more extreme the show of faith, the more wonderful the miracle."

Still, the miracle did not come. Not long after Vicki moved to Mineral Wells, Mary Elizabeth's pain became so acute that she could find no sleep, no comfort, day or night. "I would wake up in the middle of the night to hear her screaming and crying," Vicki remembers. "It was the most horrible pain I could imagine." Finally, Mary Elizabeth lost consciousness. Vicki and her brother Larry bundled her into the car and rushed her to the hospital at Carswell Air Force Base in Fort Worth. Doctors there decided her condition was too grave, and had her airlifted to a military hospital at Lackland Air Force Base in San Antonio.

In San Antonio, doctors operated on Mary Elizabeth and quickly diagnosed that she had advanced colon cancer—one of the most treatable forms of cancer if caught early. But by this time, the cancer had virtually devoured Mary Elizabeth's colon and metastasized to her liver. She had developed necrotic tissue, a condition in which tissue beneath the skin dies and rots. "When we got her to the hospital, she just started splitting open and she was black on the inside," Vicki says. "You want to talk about faith? That woman had a strong faith. She went through all of that horrible pain, because if she was steadfast, she just knew she was going to get a miracle."

In the end, Mary Elizabeth Turk did not get her miracle, at least not the one for physical healing that she was looking for. But her daughter believes something truly wonderful came out of her mother's illness. After spending six weeks in a coma at Lackland, she awoke and realized she had misplaced her trust. Not in God, but in Robert Tilton. Her faith in God was as strong—if not stronger, Vicki believes now—than it was before she became ill. "Not for a second did her faith waiver," Vicki says. "She realized that the error was not one of divine origin, it was one of human origin." Her faith was so strong, Vicki believes, that several of

Mary Elizabeth's doctors and nurses came to Vicki to tell her how deeply her mother's faith had affected them. More than once, Vicki came into her mother's room to find Mary Elizabeth with her Bible open on her lap, praying with one of her caregivers.

While Mary Elizabeth was still in the hospital, the ABC News television show *PrimeTime Live* broadcast an exposé of three noted televangelists, including Robert Tilton. In the segment aired nationally on November 21, 1991, local investigators interested in exposing spiritual frauds took the television reporters to scour Dumpsters behind Tilton's direct mail offices. With cameras rolling, they discovered that instead of praying over the handprints and pennies and prayer requests sent to Tilton by the thousands, his staff simply opened the envelopes, removed the enclosed money, and tossed out the rest.

The *PrimeTime* report was conducted with the help of the Trinity Foundation, a Dallas-based religious watchdog group that works to expose spiritual counterfeits. In the wake of the broadcast about Tilton, Ole Anthony, the group's founder, appeared on local television and asked people who believed they had been duped by Tilton to contact the foundation. Vicki was watching the news that night. She had only recently brought her mother home from the hospital to live with her in Dallas. She went to her mother's room and told her about the drive to bring Tilton to account.

Six months before she died, Mary Elizabeth Turk became the lead plaintiff in a multi-million-dollar mail fraud lawsuit against Robert Tilton. Filed in a Texas district court, the lawsuit and the *PrimeTime Live* segment prompted a federal investigation of Tilton for tax evasion and mail fraud. Within eighteen months of *PrimeTime's* broadcast, Robert Tilton's television show was canceled. His Word of Faith congregation, once thousands strong, dwindled to almost nothing. And although he ultimately settled the cases out of court, incurring no indictments and no jail time, Tilton had been disgraced and soon left town. At last report from the Trinity Foundation, Tilton lives in a five-star hotel in Miami's swanky South Beach neighborhood. And he is back on the air, this time taping from a Miami television studio. He now appears on stations in Los Angeles, Nashville, Detroit, Atlanta, and New York.

Mary Elizabeth Turk died on September 17, 1992. There was no special announcement of her death beyond the customary obituary in the local paper, the *Mineral Wells Index*. But so many people arrived for her funeral that ushers had to stand many of them in the chapel's rear. Not long after the burial, which was private, Vicki received a check for her mother's portion of the settlement—$2,000. She donated it to the Trinity Foundation, to be used to further investigate spiritual frauds.

It is hard to imagine the suffering Mary Elizabeth Turk endured for the sake of her belief in Robert Tilton's ability to bring God's healing. Vicki says she has come to understand that her mother's belief in the man was an extension of her lifelong belief in God. In her mother's mind, not to believe in Tilton would have been not to believe in God. And Mary Elizabeth simply could not do that.

Nor is it something Vicki Crenshaw could do, either. A Christian and churchgoer all of her life, she has found that the experience of witnessing her mother's struggle has somehow drawn her closer to God—as if a part of Mary Elizabeth's deep faith somehow rubbed off on her. After her mother died, Vicki felt drawn to enter the ministry, and struggled with the decision for several years. Ultimately, she became a teacher in the Dallas Independent School District, teaching art to underprivileged elementary school students. Now, she says, she sees her mother's love and trust in the faces of the children she teaches: "That's my ministry."

Despite her mother's experience, Vicki says she still believes in divine healing, just not the intercessory kind, where someone prays over the sick, or touches or anoints them. "It will just happen. Like spontaneous remission. But it will be God's choice, not yours or anybody else's."

And she is still on the lookout for bogus faith healers. Sometimes, she goes "undercover" and visits Dallas area services held by a handful of self-proclaimed healers and prophets. She most frequently drops in on the Rev. W.V. Grant. Like Tilton, Grant was disgraced in the same episode of *PrimeTime Live*, but unlike Tilton, he served time in prison for tax evasion. In early 1998, he resurfaced in Dallas, holding Sunday morning services of his "Cathedral of Compassion" church in the ballroom of a hotel in downtown Dallas.

At a service in November 2000, Vicki took a back row seat and counted one hundred people, peppered over fourteen rows of red-cushioned banquet chairs. There was an even mix of Latinos, African-Americans, and Caucasians. Some were well-dressed in dark suits and brightly printed dresses and skirts. Others were obviously down-at-the-heels. All were focused on Grant, a roundish man with slicked-back dark hair, a bright tie and matching handkerchief in his breast pocket. He strutted back and forth at the front of the room, one hand holding a microphone to his constantly moving lips, the other gesturing wildly in syncopation.

After a mish-mash sermon about giving and gaining access to God, the healings began. First, Grant singled out a rotund woman down front and asked her to tell how the cancer she had a week ago had vanished after one of Grant's services. The audience applauded as Grant crowed, "That's because when the doctors walk out, GOD walks in."

Under cover of the church bulletin she picked up at the door, Vicki took notes. She scribbled away as Grant laid his hands on the forehead of a man he said had prostate cancer. After mumbling a few unintelligible words into the microphone—a mockery of the Pentecostal practice Mary Elizabeth would have known as speaking in tongues—Grant proclaimed him "cured." The man ran up and down the aisles, praising Jesus all the way. Next came a woman Grant said had "a broken heart," courtesy of a runaway husband. With a touch of his right hand to her forehead, Grant laid her out backwards, flat on the floor, where she wept gently while people clapped enthusiastically. Then he moved on to a man he described as having a "short" leg, asking him to sit in a chair at the front of the room. The man, long and lean and with white hair, sat in profile to the audience, the leg in question placed closest to the edge of the stage. Grant knelt before him and pulled on the leg, seeming to lengthen it. As Vicki noted, the man was wearing work boots, so when Grant pulled, he actually tugged the boot down, only appearing to stretch the leg. But that didn't seem to matter to the man, who also whooped for joy and ran about thanking Grant and praising Jesus.

Grant's "healings" went on for an hour or so, but at this point Vicki had all she could take. In the elevator down to the hotel lobby, she fought back tears. In the rainy parking lot, she spoke in a rush. "They know their target audience, and they know what buttons to push, and they do it in the name of God," she said, putting the key into the door of her car. Inside, hanging from the rearview mirror, is a little bookmark that reads, "There are no facts, only interpretations." As she pulled onto the freeway, she continued, "That just drives me nuts. If those people really have those terrible problems, they are being led along this little rosy path that everything is just going to be fine, and it is not." A second later, she added, "I can see how my mother was pulled in."

Later she drove west on Interstate 80, making the trip to Mineral Wells, where she still keeps her mother's house pretty much as it was when she left for the hospital—dime-store paintings of the New England countryside on the walls, crocheted doilies on the tables, worn linoleum on the floors. She has converted her mother's bedroom into a sewing room, but says she seldom uses it. "It hurts to go in," she explains.

In honor of her mother's memory, she has tried single-handedly to revive Mineral Wells's struggling downtown. In the shadow of the Baker Hotel, a huge, Jazz Age brick structure now boarded up for lack of a buyer, she has opened an art gallery for the town's seniors and a small resale shop full of glitter nail polish and patent leather platform shoes for the local teens. She has also established the Mary Elizabeth Turk Foundation Scholarship Fund, which makes a small award to a Mineral Wells high school student every year. Vicki's dream is to make this town, where the biggest attractions are a washing machine museum and a bat sanctuary, as beloved by others as it was by her mother. "I want a legacy that will be positive and upbeat, and not to have her be remembered for being victimized," she says. "That was a tragedy, but it was not the end-all of who she was."

But despite her anger and frustration at "false prophets," Vicki does not disparage the people who truly believe in gifts of the Spirit. "To do so would be unfair and against my deepest beliefs," she says. "I love an old Eastern proverb that states, 'Walk softly when you enter the realm of another's religion. Remember, God was there before you.'"

They Shall Lay Hands on the Sick and They Shall Recover

A Brief History of Faith Healing

Mary Elizabeth Turk had to look no further than the leather-bound Bible she kept at her side to find examples of the miraculous healing she desired. Both the Old and New Testaments are filled with instances of sudden and wondrous healings, so much so that the religious scholar R.J.S. Barrett-Lennard has commented that ancient Christian texts are more concerned with illness and healing than any other religious writings from the same period. The bulk of these biblical healings stem from the ministry of Jesus. The Gospels record more than forty of his healing miracles, including restoring the blind, the crippled, and the leprous, and raising people from the dead. Jesus is said to have healed the sick and infirm right up to his death, even as he carried the cross on his back to Golgotha.

Almost as soon as Christ was crucified, his apostles began traveling the known world to spread his good news, and many of his followers performed healing miracles wherever they went. In the third chapter of Acts, Peter encounters a lame beggar and tells him, "Silver and gold have I none; but such as I have I give thee: In the name of Jesus Christ of Nazareth, rise up and walk" (verse 6). The man does. Peter goes on to restore a paralyzed man and raise a woman from the dead, while Paul, too, is credited with healing a cripple. There are also mass healings associated with the apostles, as when Peter's shadow cures all the ills it falls upon (Acts 5:15), and when scraps of cloth that once touched Paul cured the sick (Acts 19:11). The apostle James exhorts his fellow Christians not only to pray for healing, but also to expect it. "Is any sick among you ?" he writes to the followers of Christ. "Let him call for the elders of the church; and let them pray over him, anointing him with oil in the name of the Lord; and the prayer of faith shall save the sick, and the Lord shall raise him up" (James 5:14–15).

By the time the Christian church began its formal organization, the works of the apostles had firmly established healing as an integral part of the faith. In the latter half of the second century, Ireneaus, a bishop in the church in Gaul, wrote that "some [Christians] heal the sick by laying their hands upon them and they are made whole,"[1] and told of personally witnessing the raising of the dead after fasting and prayer. Origen, a major theologian in the third-century Greek Church, wrote of numerous people being cured by Christians when other means had failed. Whenever and wherever these healings occurred, they were held up as proof of the divinity of Christ and of his anointing by God, and were responsible for converting countless people to Christianity. By the third century, healings were so much a part of early Christian practice that laymen were specially trained for the office, ultimately prompting one bishop to complain that these healers outnumbered the priests.

The conversion of Constantine to Christianity in the early fourth century lent a legitimacy to Christian faith healings. At this time, healings continued to be performed as they always had, with the laying on of hands, anointing with oil, and sometimes with the healer breathing on the sick or wetting them with holy water. Historians Palladius and Athanasius wrote about the desert fathers who retreated into the Egyptian desert to live the Christian life, often as hermits. Some of these monks were credited with miraculous cures. In the Middle Ages, pilgrims made long journeys by land and sea to the Holy Land, many of them intent on seeing relics of saints that were said to hold healing powers—perhaps a bone, a piece of wood, or a scrap of cloth.

From the Middle Ages to the Enlightenment, faith healers wandered through England and Europe, some claiming to cure by a relic in their possession, others relying on nothing but a touch of their hands. The state of medicine at this time was primitive; no one had yet seen a bacterium or knew of the existence of genes, and belief in faith healing was common. Several faith healers became quite well known and successful in their trade. In England in the late 1600s, a healer called "Greatraks" was widely known for his ability to heal through what he claimed was a God-given power, prompting one of his contemporaries to write, "Catholics and Protestants visited him from every part, all believing that power from heaven was in his hands."[2] He was in good company. Three hundred years before, Philip the Fair, King of France, was known for being able to cure scrofula and other skin diseases with a touch of his hand.

Faith healing came to America in the seventeenth century with the Society of Friends, or Quakers as they were more derisively called because of their habit of shaking ecstatically during worship. The Quakers were founded by George Fox, an itinerant

English preacher well known for his healing ministry. When Fox prayed for the sick, he practiced the laying on of hands. Fox and his followers believed that faith healing was the work of God, not of man, but they did not discourage the use of doctors and medicine. Fox traveled widely in the American colonies and the Caribbean; and wherever he went, he told of the healing miracles he had witnessed, and attempted to cure more of the local sick. A "Book of Miracles," which was discovered among his papers after his death in 1691, described more than 150 healing miracles, many with which he had been involved. In America, the Quakers continued to practice the laying on of hands into the nineteenth century.

The Brethren, another early American religious group, hearkened back to the Bible to revive the practice of anointing the sick with oil. In their writings, the Brethren—also known as "the Dunkers" for their practice of full-immersion baptism—described their belief in anointing as a means of producing miraculous cures. When the Brethren ultimately divided into four distinct denominations, each one took with it an emphasis on divine healing.

In the early 1800s a spirit of revivalism swept the young United States, giving rise to a new fervor for God's miracles, especially for healing. The "burned-over" district of western New York—so called because of the repeated waves of religious fervor it fostered—gave rise to many new groups that embraced faith healing, including the Mormons, the Adventists, and the Shakers. The Shakers believed the power to heal had been handed down by Christ to his disciples and was in practice today in the "true Christian church," which they believed was their own. Healings through the laying on of hands by the Shakers' founder, Mother Ann Lee, were routinely reported, with many of the recovered submitting affidavits as to their divinely restored health. But unlike the Quakers, the Shakers scorned the use of traditional doctors and medicine, relying instead on strict hygiene and herbal remedies. Ultimately, the Shakers and their way of life died out.

The same fate befell the Noyesites, followers of John Humphrey Noyes, who established the utopian Oneida Community in upstate New York in 1841. Noyes taught that disease was the direct consequence of personal sin and the influence of evil spirits. His group expected miraculous cures to occur in their lives because the Bible promised them so . By the early 1880s, the Oneida Community dissolved. Noyes died in Canada in 1886, and the greatest legacy his followers left was the establishment of the Oneida Silver Company.

Divine healing was also a part of the Mormon tradition at the time of its founding in the 1830s. The Mormon prophet, Joseph Smith, was known to pray for the healing of the sick, and sometimes sent anointed handkerchiefs to sufferers far away. His followers credited him with curing many cases of disease, like measles and fevers. But, like the Quakers, Smith never turned his back on doctors and medicines, both of which he described as being endowed with healing properties by God.

In the early days of their church, Seventh-day Adventists also believed in divine healing. They were originally part of the Millerite movement—a millennialist group that predicted Christ would return October 22, 1844. The Adventists split from the Millerites after that day came and went, an event known as the "Great Disappointment." Under their leader, Ellen Gould White, miraculous cures and healings were a routine part of Adventist meetings. Following the example of the apostles described in James 5, White anointed sick persons with oil and laid her hands upon them in healing prayer. And, like the Shakers, she taught that reliance on doctors was a denial of God. Today, Seventh-day Adventists have shifted their focus to healthful living, and maintain a number of medical facilities worldwide.

But it wasn't until the Holiness Movement of the nineteenth century that faith healing became a major pillar of any group or sect's theology. The Holiness Movement emphasized personal perfection, called "sanctification," through the supernatural intervention of God in people's lives. This intervention of God came to be called the "baptism of the Holy Spirit" and was partially derived from the experience of the apostles on the first Pentecost, when the Holy Spirit moved among them as a wind and brought forth many signs and wonders said to herald the last days before the coming of Christ. Early proponents of the Holiness Movement described sanctification as there for the taking—a kind of "name it and claim it" reservoir of health and prosperity. And if someone failed to be healed of disease, it was seen as his or her own fault, perhaps the result of some hidden personal sin.

The first American preacher to wed the Holiness Movement with a focus on divine healing was Ethan O. Allen. In 1846, while he was in his twenties, Allen believed he was healed of tuberculosis through the prayers of Methodist lay leaders. He began a ministry of praying for the sick, becoming the first American preacher to make faith healing his primary goal. For fifty years, Allen traveled the eastern United States, preaching and praying for the sick in poor houses, camp meetings, and churches. A number of people who credited him with their healings also took up faith healing as their ministry, and, as they too began to travel, the faith healing movement spread.

One of Allen's disciples was an African-American woman named Mrs. Elizabeth Mix. Better educated and more articulate than Allen, she formulated a principle of the healing movement still in place today—that the person seeking faith healing must not only believe that God is healing them, but also must act as if they believe it. So, if the lame seek to be healed, they must try to walk; if the deaf seek to be healed, they must try to hear.

Another of Allen's followers, Charles Cullis, took the American form of faith healing to an international audience. Cullis was a well-respected Boston doctor, and founded a publishing house that printed and circulated tracts and pamphlets on divine healing. He held regular healing services in his house and founded a faith-healing home. When, in 1870, he seemed to have cured a young woman of a brain tumor that had incapacitated her for months, clergy in the Holiness community took notice. Cullis went on a tour of Europe, further spreading the Holiness movement's philosophy that the power of divine healing rests with the individual's responsibility to live a Christian life. Newspapers and magazines, which had never paid much attention to claims of miraculous healings, were suddenly scrambling to cover Cullis's camp meetings, held annually in Massachusetts and Maine. These stories spread news of healing miracles across the United States and around the world. In 1887, R. Kelso Carter, a proponent of faith healing, wrote in *Century Magazine*, "True or False, there is no belief rising more swiftly before the churches everywhere than that of Divine Healing."[3] By the end of the century, faith healing was well-established and accepted in the minds of many Christians of all backgrounds and denominations—so much so that a thesis entitled "Faith Healing: A Defense, of the Lord, Thy Healer" was submitted and accepted for a bachelor of divinity degree at Yale Divinity School. Faith healing had become a topic of serious discussion and inquiry in the American mainstream.

Perhaps the nineteenth-century religious movement with the most controversial legacy of healing is the First Church of Christ,

Scientist, more commonly known as the Christian Science Church. Founded by Mary Baker Eddy, daughter of New England farmers, its healing practices have been the subject of numerous court cases almost since the church's founding in 1879. Christian Science rests on a belief in faith healing—or, as the church prefers, divine healing. Christian Scientists believe all illness, disease, and pain are illusions and serve only to separate man from "Mind," or God. Christian Scientists are strongly encouraged to rely exclusively on prayer to heal the sick, though church officials have lately emphasized writings of Mrs. Eddy's that seem to say church members may seek out medical care, if they wish. But usually, when an ailment persists, Christian Scientists employ "practitioners," who are nonmedical persons trained and licensed by the church to pray for the healing of others. Christian Scientists tout their reported healings—to date, more than 60,000 of them—in the personal testimonies of church members in *The Christian Science Journal*, a monthly church periodical, and *The Christian Science Sentinel*, a church weekly.

Of all the faith healers of the nineteenth century, it was Carrie Judd Montgomery who had the most influence on the movement in the twentieth century. Montgomery, an Episcopalian by birth, was healed of a severe disability by Elizabeth Mix in 1879. One year later, she published an account of her healing under the title "The Prayer of Faith," and was soon traveling around the world as a proponent of faith healing. She became allied with the Christian Missionary Alliance, a Holiness denomination, and established faith-healing homes in California, including one in Oakland where she held a healing service weekly for twenty-five years. Montgomery became the first woman evangelist to travel from coast to coast to spread the gospel of divine healing. Her husband, George Montgomery, attended services at the Azusa Street

Mission, where the Pentecostal revival was born, and he accepted the gifts of the Holy Spirit being taught and experienced there. Two years later, his wife had the same experience and began speaking in tongues. She later allied her ministry with the Assemblies of God, becoming the first living link from the Holiness movement to the Pentecostal movement. Much of what Montgomery preached is still found among the theology of Pentecostal faith healers today—that in order to be healed, Christians must believe both that they are healed (and act accordingly) and accept the entire Bible as the literal, and therefore true, word of God.

Aimee Semple McPherson took Montgomery's example and improved upon it. Like Montgomery, she preached healing across the country, making eight transcontinental trips between 1918 and 1923. McPherson preached that Christ was the "Great Physician," capable of curing all ailments. In 1922, she took her message to the airwaves, becoming the first woman to preach on the radio. Soon, she purchased her own station. At the height of her popularity, she led twenty-one healing services a week at her 5,300-seat Angelus Temple in Los Angeles and published two national periodicals. Today, her ministry has evolved into the International Church of the Foursquare Gospel, with some 1.8 million members worldwide.

From the end of the nineteenth century through the Azusa Street Revival of 1906, literally thousands of Holiness congregations and dozens of Holiness sects dotted the American religious landscape, especially in the South and Southwest. A majority of them emphasized divine healing, but some carried it to the extreme and taught that resorting to doctors and medicines demonstrated a lack of faith in Christ. Many of these tiny groups have since been swallowed up by larger, more mainstream denominations, but many still survive, including the Church of the Nazarene and the Pilgrim Holiness Church. When the fever of Azusa Street spread, numerous independent Pentecostal congregations popped up, too, many with an emphasis on healing. The largest of these were Church of God denominations. Today, just including the Holiness and Church of God denominations, there are millions of believers in faith healing.

In the middle of the twentieth century, Americans were preoccupied with World War II, and there was a general decline in church attendance as men went overseas and women went to work. But in the calm after World War II, the country again began to turn toward the spiritual. People returned to church by the thousands, driving church membership rolls up. In what religion scholars have come to call "The Third Great Awakening," faith healing was to play an active, and controversial, role.

By the 1940s and 50s, the essential belief in faith healing had changed very little. Proponents of faith healing still widely preached that it was there to be claimed by any Christian who stood open to the gifts of the Spirit. But what had changed was the stage on which faith healing stood. The use of radio as a tool of evangelism, pioneered by Aimee Semple McPherson, became widespread in the 1930s. William Branham and later Oral Roberts were among the first faith-healing evangelists to use the airwaves to spread the testimonies of the healing miracles they performed. Branham brought faith healing a new respectability when, in 1951, he famously cured William Upshaw, a United States Congressman from California, of a crippling disability he had had since birth.

Television brought these men and their deeds even more fame, as audiences could now actually see the healing miracles these new "televangelists" claimed in God's name—the crippled throwing away their crutches, the blind opening their eyes, the deaf shouting that they could hear. Television launched faith healing far from its Pentecostal and Holiness platforms, as healers like Oral Roberts, Kathryn Kuhlman, and Jimmy Swaggart took the soundstage. Roberts, perhaps, did the most to further the notoriety of faith healing; his television show reached millions of people every week—many of whom had never before seen faith healing—and became the number one syndicated television show for almost thirty years in a row. In addition, he undertook to bring faith healing to a prime time television audience, and did remarkably well. His program, *Expect a Miracle*, reached 64 million people a week, and included an eleven-minute sermon and a prayer for the healing of the sick. Roberts also brought faith healing right into the heart of mainstream Protestantism when, in 1968, he left his Holiness roots to align himself and his vast ministry with the United Methodist Church. By 1965, he estimated that more than half his audiences were non-Pentecostal Christians. The City of Faith Medical and Research Center, which Roberts opened in Tulsa, Oklahoma, in 1981, was the first major medical facility in the world with the purpose of treating illness equally through prayer and medicine.

Another televangelist who transplanted faith healing from its Pentecostal and charismatic roots was Kathryn Kuhlman. Though her background was in the Pentecostal movement, she focused her ministry, founded in 1946, on reaching mainline Protestants. In 1950, she preached from a pulpit in Carnegie Music Hall in Pittsburgh, Pennsylvania, and made it her home for the next two decades. When she began holding weekly healing services at the Shriner Auditorium in Los Angeles, she attracted 7,000 people a week.

Faith healing has become even more widespread in the last twenty-five years as Pentecostal and charismatic beliefs have seeped steadily into the more traditionally mainstream denominations. Today, it is not hard to find a Presbyterian, Methodist, Episcopal, or Catholic church with a regular healing service that may include the laying on of hands, intercessory prayer, anointing, or some other form of original healing ritual, like the lighting of memorial candles or the construction of a quilt.

Judaism, too, is currently experiencing a healing movement that includes healing services in synagogues and the creation of about twenty "Jewish healing centers" throughout the United States. While Judaism has always included a belief in God's power to heal, this movement is new in that it employs Jewish prayers and traditions to bring about not only physical healing, but also spiritual wholeness.

It is hard to measure exactly how widespread the belief in faith healing is today. It is somewhat easier to estimate the number of charismatic Christians, a label that originated with a lay-led revival and is used to describe Christians of any denomination who believe in God's bestowal of spiritual gifts, such as speaking in tongues, prophesying, and especially healing. In *World Christian Encyclopedia*, David Barrett figures that by 1988 there were 359 million charismatic Christians worldwide. That would make it the fastest growing religious movement in the world. Other scholars assert the movement has tripled three times in the last decade.

There have been few large, national surveys on belief in faith healing, and only a handful of smaller studies. But even those are telling. A *USA Today* poll conducted in 1996 found that 56 percent of respondents believed they had been cured of an illness as a result of prayer or other religious practice. A *Time* magazine poll conducted in the same year found that 77 percent of American adults believed that God sometimes intervenes to cure people with serious illnesses. However, the same poll found that only 28 percent believed that faith healers could cure through their own faith or personal touch. And the University of Chicago's National Opinion Research Council estimates that almost 20 million Americans report having had some mystical experience, including healing.

To date, the broadest and most specific survey on belief in faith healing and other forms of nonmedical treatment was performed in the mid-1980s by Dr. Meredith McGuire and her colleagues at the Alternative Healing Systems Project at Montclair State College. Over four years, Dr. McGuire set out to study the alternative health beliefs and practices among suburbanites—both Christians and others—in northern New Jersey. Her findings shattered some stereotypes about those who employ nonmedical healing practices. For one thing, belief in nonmedical healing rituals and practices is not limited to people with low incomes or low levels of education; the bulk of McGuire's respondents were from middle-income backgrounds and had attained some level of higher education. McGuire and her team identified more than 130 different groups of healers from five broad healing types—everything from Transcendental Meditation to Christian Science and other, nontraditional forms of treatment. The study also found that most of the alternative healing methods employed by the subjects were not performed by specialized healers or paid for in any way, but were undertaken by the subjects for themselves or others.

Perhaps more important, McGuire's study showed that the definition of "healing" means more than physical restoration to most people who employ nonmedical treatment. She and her staff heard people tell of restored relationships, increased personal insight, and new ideas and hopes for the future. Suffering was reduced by the sense of taking control of the illness and seeking the help and support of others. "When successful," McGuire wrote, "healing often creates the sense of becoming enlarged—not reduced—by the experience of illness."[4]

That is certainly what happened to Michelle Potter, a transplanted New Yorker from a Catholic and Lutheran background, who never let the relentlessness of cancer erode the solidity of her faith.

THREE

Tender Mercies

The Story of Michelle Potter

Michelle and Chris Potter proved the old adage that opposites attract. While he was a pale blue-eyed blonde, she was a shiny brunette with sparkling brown eyes. Where she loved to plan fabulous meals a week in advance, he enjoyed her cooking as much as her joke that he would eat anything she put in front of him, even if it was dog food. In conversation with others, Chris was reflective and quiet, often preferring to listen rather than talk, while Michelle could walk up to strangers, dazzle them with her high-beam smile, and, in a few minutes of chat, make them feel she had known them all their lives.

Michelle and Chris were married on August 3, 1985, in a Catholic church in Michelle's hometown of Niskayuna, New York, a small town outside of Albany. Both their families were there, looking on with wide smiles and lots of tears. After a honeymoon in Hawaii, the couple settled in Buffalo, New York, with Chris going to work everyday as an electrical designer and Michelle going to work in the billing department of a children's hospital.

For two years Michelle and Chris tried unsuccessfully to have a child. Finally, Courtney Ann Potter was born in 1992. Three

years later, in 1995, the couple moved to Kingwood, Texas, a leafy
green suburb of Houston, where Chris's company had relocated.
Within a year, they were happily awaiting the birth of their second
child.

Seven months into the pregnancy, Michelle began to experience some vaginal bleeding. Her concerned doctor ordered a Pap
smear, a swabbing of the cervix to test for abnormalities. When
the results came back, Michelle called Chris at work. Seven-and-
a-half months pregnant, Michelle had ovarian cancer. The
bleeding had been caused by a cancerous mass pushing down
into her uterus and intestines.

Michelle DiPippo Potter was one of the 20,700 women
ovarian cancer strikes each year. At the time, she was thirty-four
years old. Chances of developing ovarian cancer increase with
age, and it is most common among women with a family history
of ovarian cancer, post-menopausal women, and women who
have never had children. Michelle fit none of these categories.

But one category Michelle did fit was fighter. At five-foot
two and weighing in at just over 100 pounds—even less at the
peak of her illness—Michelle was a world-class, heavyweight
champion. She battled her cancer with every form of medical
treatment she could find, both established and experimental,
looking for a cure. At the same time she fought her cancer with
drugs, she fought it with a couple of rounds of faith healing. But
the one thing Michelle's friends and family say she never had to
fight for was her faith—an absolute faith that God could and
would heal her, according to what she saw as his own mysterious
plan.

"The desire and the belief that the miracle could happen
never went away," Chris said one evening at his kitchen table.
The house was quiet around him, with the girls put to bed and

Michelle gone. "She wanted to live. She wanted to be there for her children and be there for her husband."

Michelle's initial diagnosis was made in January 1997. A few days later, her bleeding became so severe that Chris awoke one night to find her standing in the bathtub in a pool of blood. He rushed her to the hospital, where doctors wanted to surgically remove the cancer and start her on chemotherapy as soon as possible. But first, they had to deliver Michelle's baby. On February 3, one week after Michelle's diagnosis, doctors performed a Caesarian section on Michelle, delivering her baby six weeks before its due date. Then, in the same surgical session, they removed a cancerous growth the size of a child's fist from Michelle's abdomen. They also had to perform a complete hysterectomy and a partial bowel reconstruction to repair some of the damage done by the cancer.

In the middle of the pain and discomfort caused by the cancer and then her surgery, Michelle focused on her joy in her new baby girl, Kaitlin Marie. Born six weeks prematurely, Kaitlin had to be kept in the hospital. She couldn't suckle, and doctors were worried about her immune system, so they performed a very painful spinal tap. But if the new baby had Chris's blonde hair and blue eyes, she also had Michelle's fighting personality. When she was two-and-a-half weeks old, Kaitlin was finally pronounced ready to go home with her family.

After Kaitlin's birth, Michelle's prognosis was good—the surgeon had removed as much cancer as she could, to the point that there was just a peppering of cancer cells remaining across her diaphragm. Her doctors were optimistic that, with six months of chemotherapy, she could be cancer-free. She spent a year in remission, staying home to take care of the new baby and Courtney, who was now five years old and starting school. Things looked as if they were going to be fine. Speaking to her mother by telephone about her progress, Michelle said, "Mom, I am going to beat this. God is going to help me, and we are going to win."

But the cancer was stubborn. It was back by September 1998. Michelle started another six-month round of chemo, and then had more surgery to remove a cancerous blockage in her small intestine. Still, the cancer persisted. Finally, in May 1999, Michelle had run through all of the most successful, "first-line" treatments available in Houston. Her doctors told her they were sorry, but there was little more they could do for her.

At the time of Michelle's diagnosis, the Potters attended a Catholic church in Kingwood, but their attendance was sporadic— a Sunday once or twice a month. Michelle had been raised Catholic; and, although Chris's family was from the American Baptist Church, a mainline Protestant denomination, he attended the Catholic church with his wife. Still, the Potters found it diffi- cult to find their own niche in Kingwood's Catholic community, which numbered thousands of member families.

While Kaitlin was still a baby, a neighbor told Michelle of a mothers' support group and suggested Michelle drop in. Called Mothers of Pre-Schoolers (or MOPS, for short), the group met at Kingwood's Christ the King Lutheran Church, a congregation with about 1,200 members that was affiliated with the Lutheran Church Missouri Synod, a mainline Protestant denomination.

Michelle began attending one of the group's monthly meet- ings, and almost immediately felt at home. In time, she met Beth Fluker, who, with her husband, Tom, and infant son, Brent, were members of Christ the King. The two women liked each other immediately, and it wasn't long before Michelle told Beth about her cancer and confided that she didn't have a priest she felt comfortable talking with about it.

Beth was deeply affected by Michelle's situation. She couldn't help but see herself in her new friend's place. Worried that Michelle didn't have a pastor she could talk to, Beth pointed her to her own pastor, the Rev. Al Doering. Pastor Al told Michelle that if she ever needed someone to talk to, his door, and the doors of Christ the King, were always open to her and her family. Michelle and Chris were touched by his concern, and they soon became regulars at Christ the King's Sunday morning services. In the fall of 2000, the Potters became members of the church.

Michelle made many new friends through MOPS, both with young women like Beth, Terry Magnani and Patty Kalass—all mothers of small children, like herself—and with older women like Polly Phillips, an "empty-nester," who served as a mentor to the younger women in the group. Soon they were sharing confidences as well as recipes, tears as well as laughter, and were supporting each other in their faith. But everyone who knew Michelle at this time said she never laid her struggle with cancer out on the table for all to see and worry about. Instead, even when she was sick with side effects from her chemo or worried about the success of her treatment, she always placed her friends' cares and worries before her own.

"I asked Michelle to talk to me when she was down, to talk to me when she was worried or scared," Terry said, "but she always held back. She wanted to protect her friends from feeling sad or hurt. She didn't want anyone to be dragged down by her." Patty added, "She always said, 'Don't stop telling me your own problems, because when you tell them to me, I feel like I am not sick.'" Patty and Terry shared a look, and then Patty said, "She felt like she was going to get a miracle. She was waiting for the Lord."

There was one friend, Karen Cagney, a nearby neighbor to whom Michelle could unburden herself if she wanted, and she often did. Sometimes Michelle would call before eight in the morning and say how, when she woke up, her first thought was, "I have cancer," and she wanted just to pull the covers over her head. Then she'd say, "Thank you, God, for one more day," get out of bed, and keep going. On the telephone, Michelle would tell Karen, "I just don't think I am going to die from this." Karen recalled, "She'd say 'I really feel that this is a mission for me, that I am supposed to get through this and then help other women get through the same thing.' We'd say how when this was all over, she was going to have to go on *Oprah*, and then we'd laugh. Then she'd ask, 'Do you think this is denial, or is this my faith?'"

When doctors in Houston gave Michelle the bad news in the spring of 1999, she was not ready to give up. One of her doctors told her of a clinical trial for a new drug treatment for ovarian cancer underway at the National Institute of Health in Bethesda, Maryland. In August 1999, Michelle began traveling from Kingwood to Bethesda one week every month to be part of the trial. On these trips, she stayed with her younger sister, Pati, who at about the same time was planning to move from New Jersey to Centerville, Virginia, with her husband, David, and their two children.

The two sisters were very close. As children, they had worked together in their grandmother's card store and had learned the rosary from the older woman, a very devout Catholic. On Sundays, the whole family went to Mass, and the two girls attended catechism class and made their first confessions and first communions together, donning white dresses that looked like miniature wedding gowns. Even after they were grown, Pati looked up to Michelle and wanted to be just like her big sister. "She was my best friend," Pati said.

For the next year, Michelle continued to travel to Bethesda each month for a week of treatment. Doctors at NIH placed a port in her chest—an open tube through which the new medicine could flow directly into her bloodstream. While she was away from home, Michelle's mother, Naomi, or Chris's mother, Jean, would come to Houston to take care of Courtney and Kaitlin. After Michelle's return, the grandmothers would stay for another week or so, to help out until she could get back on her feet. Two or three days after coming home, Michelle would be back to her regular activities— helping Courtney with her schoolwork, playing with Kaitlin, grocery shopping, cooking, and going to church. She would not let the cancer, or the nausea and other side effects her treatment caused, deprive her family of the love and care she wanted to give them. And when the month was over and it was time to go to Bethesda again, she hated to go. "Michelle hated that people's lives had to be changed around for her," Chris said. "She hated that we were taking the grandmothers away from the grandfathers. And the treatment itself was nothing in comparison to her having to be away from the girls for a whole week. She called home every night."

Each time Michelle went off to Bethesda, her friends at home did what they could to support her. They organized telephone prayer chains and arranged group prayers at significant times, like at the exact moment Michelle would lie down for a CAT scan, or during the time she was having a meeting with her doctors. Karen Cagney put together a kind of "love package" for Michelle before each of her trips—a large envelope filled with smaller envelopes to be opened by Michelle, one for each day she was away from home. They were filled with cards, personal notes, devotional readings, and bits of Scriptures and prayers. Each of these things was designed so that Michelle, making the long trip to Bethesda on her own, would feel less alone.

The trips to Bethesda were draining, but they were also paying off. Michelle's cancer was getting smaller—shrinking to about the size of a pea at one point—and Michelle was gaining weight and feeling better. It was a time of hope for everyone who knew her.

But in August 2000, Michelle's routine blood test indicated that the cancer was gaining strength, in effect becoming immune to the new drugs. Her doctors tried two more cycles of the new chemo, but by November it was clear the cancer was growing. There was one more possibility, another clinical trial of another new drug; but the trial could not begin until March 2001. Not wanting to wait four months for more treatment, Michelle decided to stay home and try one of the less effective, "second-line" treatments available to her in Houston, and submitted herself to more chemo in January 2001. But by March, halfway through the treatment, she showed no improvement. Her doctors again told her they were sorry. But Michelle, still fighting for her life with her family, decided to fly back to Bethesda and NIH for the new clinical trial.

That spring, while Michelle was again flying back and forth to Bethesda on a monthly basis, members of Christ the King Lutheran Church felt they wanted to do more for Michelle than pray for her on Sunday mornings or at home on their own. The church's associate pastor, the Rev. Doyle Theimer, had come to know Michelle, Chris, and the girls; and he wanted to hold a special service of healing for her. He had never held a formal healing service before—the traditional forms of faith healing are not a routine part of the Lutheran ministry—but he felt increasingly compelled to petition God for Michelle's healing in a more focused, organized fashion.

In early March, Pastor Doyle telephoned the Potters and proposed that they hold a healing service for Michelle at the church. Anyone she wanted to invite could be there—friends, family, and neighbors of any faith. The Potters were also unfamiliar with this kind of healing service. Chris's American Baptist upbringing had not encompassed any kind of ritualized faith healing, and neither had Michelle's Catholic background, though both were raised to believe that healing was one of God's gifts. However, in the two years that they had been attending Christ the King, they had come to trust the congregation and its leaders entirely, and readily agreed to the service. "We never even thought about its being unusual, or in any way frightening or strange," Chris said. "We just had a good feeling about it and said, yes, let's do this."

On March 15, about thirty of Michelle's friends and family gathered in Christ the King's main sanctuary to ask God to heal Michelle. Some of those gathered were from Christ the King, others knew Michelle from MOPS, and others knew her from the neighborhood. They sat in a circle of chairs beneath a ceiling pierced by a skylight with a view of the clouds above. Pastor Doyle led them all in prayers and songs, and then read from Mark, Acts, and Psalm 103:

> Bless the LORD, O my soul, and all that is within me bless his
>   holy name.
> Bless the LORD, O my soul, and forget not all his benefits:
> Who forgiveth all thine iniquities; who healeth all thy diseases;
> Who redeemeth thy life from destruction; who crowneth thee
>   with lovingkindness and tender mercies. . . (v. 1–4).

After his reading, Pastor Doyle explained to the group that they were here to pray for Michelle's healing. He explained how any time people prayed for someone, that person was blessed.

Pastor Doyle then moved behind Michelle and placed his hand on her right shoulder. Chris came around behind his wife, knelt down, and placed his hand on her left shoulder. Pastor Doyle bowed his head and said a prayer. He asked God to heal Michelle, to strengthen her faith, and to fill her with his love. He then invited anyone else who wanted to come up and lay hands on Michelle and pray for her. Most people prayed from their chairs; but several people came forward, including twelve-year-old Alex Gentry, who asked simply, "Please, God, heal Mrs. Potter."

After the service, Michelle told Beth that when she was in the middle of the circle of chairs, she opened her eyes and saw herself surrounded by the love of her best friends. She was encompassed in a circle of love and healing. She said she felt the presence of God. And on the drive home that night, a butterfly alighted on the windshield of the Potters' car. It was dark outside and to see a butterfly at night seemed a rare and wonderful thing. Michelle pointed it out to Chris, and they took it as a sign from God that she had been blessed. Later, at home, Chris gave Michelle a marker and said, "Write it on the calendar. Today is the day you are healed."

Shortly before the healing service at Christ the King, one of Michelle's neighbors had told her about a Catholic priest who was holding a healing Mass in Kingwood. Chris stayed home with the girls so Michelle could go

That experience was also something new for Michelle. When she came home, she told Chris how the priest asked those who were in need of healing to come forward for a laying on of his hands. When the priest touched her, she fell backward in a kind of a faint—what charismatic Christians know as being "slain" in the Holy Spirit. She lay on the floor for a few minutes afterward, not feeling any pain, but feeling a sense of well-being pass over her.

Afterward, she told Chris, the priest instructed that, if they wanted God to heal them, they should proclaim that he had done so. Chris and Michelle agreed to think and act as if she had been truly, finally healed.

But by May 2001, there was no change in her condition. Michelle heard from the doctors in Bethesda what she had already heard twice from the doctors in Houston—there is nothing else we can do. Michelle went home to Kingwood, to her family, to wait for what she saw as God's will.

Michelle battled one of the most aggressive, most feared forms of cancer for four-and-a-half years. She fought hard because she had a lot to lose—two beautiful little girls and a husband, a mother, a father, a sister, and a brother, all of whom she loved very much.

And throughout her fight, Michelle's friends and family said she never showed any anger at God, never complained to them of the burden he had given her. Beth had asked her once, "Michelle, aren't you mad, aren't you angry with God for letting this happen to you?" Beth remembered Michelle's response. "Boy, she put me in my place. She told me God didn't do this to her, but he was going to help her deal with it. That's why I can sit here and talk about it without crying; she just gave us all so much strength. Even when she would get down, she would say, 'I hope God doesn't think I am giving up on him.'"

Michelle's mother, Naomi Powell, said giving up on God was something Michelle never even considered. Her daughter's faith, she said, was not something she learned in Sunday school, but was a gift from God—a gift he sent to help her cope. "It was always there," Naomi said. "She always felt he would give her strength, and he did, for four-and-a-half years." Polly Phillips, Michelle's mentor in MOPS, prayed frequently with her; and she, too, said she never saw her faith falter. "Sometimes when faith is all we have, we discover that faith is all we need," she said.

The depth of Michelle's reserves astonished her sister, Pati. "It's not as though a miracle had happened before, and she could point to that as confirmation of her belief in miracles," she said. "But never once did we talk about if she died. It just seemed even in the darkest times, she always had hope. I think she knew that if you don't have hope and you don't have faith, you have nothing."

Chris's mother, Jean Potter, said Michelle once confided to her that, in a really dark moment, she had yelled at God, had cried and screamed at him. "She was just so frustrated with every-thing, at not seeing results, at not knowing what to do, and she was asking God for an answer," Jean said. "We are all human, and no matter how much we love God, we all have anger." Michelle allowed Chris to see this part of her battle, too, but only in rare glimpses. "She did break down a few times and cry and say this wasn't fair," he said. "But it would be late at night, when the day was done, and she never did that in front of anyone but me, because she didn't want to bother other people. We both tried to make life as normal as we could, and in the daily routine there was just no time for that. But at night, it would hit you."

Most of the time, Chris watched with awe as Michelle's faith helped her through. She had always believed in God and in Jesus Christ, but he did not know how strong her belief was until it was tested. "When she stood up in church one Sunday and gave her testimony about her fight with cancer, I was just shocked," he said. "I just didn't know that her faith was that strong." Now, in hindsight, he thinks her faith grew right along with her cancer. And Michelle's blossoming faith affected him and the children, too. "Because of her sickness, all of our faith grew," he said. "Through all of that, your family can't help but grow in its faith."

Michelle once asked Karen Cagney if her friend thought her hope was faith or denial. Karen knows the answer now. "It is easy to have a lot of faith when everything is going with you," she said, "but Michelle's faith was exceptional, because she had everything going against her." And that faith, Karen believes, was a gift, not a skill. "I don't think you can be taught the kind of faith she knew. It was like breathing to her. She didn't have to think about whether she was going to have faith or whether she was going to fight. They were natural to her. And I think that was one of the greatest gifts God gave her."

In the last month before Michelle's death, she and her sister were talking by telephone. Pati was discussing the possibilities of Michelle's returning to NIH to try one more experimental treatment—one in which doctors would grow a kind of vaccine from tissue taken from Michelle's body. The treatment would take at least five weeks to prepare. Pati believes Michelle could never say to her, "I am too ill to make the trip," or "I don't think I have five weeks left." So Michelle said, "I just don't think I have the strength to get on the plane," Pati remembered. "She was very subtle, and she wanted to protect the people she loved from any pain on her behalf. So I said, 'Michelle, what are you telling me?' And she said, 'It is in God's hands now.'"

In the first week of August, Michelle became so ill that she had to be hospitalized. In a meeting with her surgeon, she did not ask what further treatments were available, but instead thanked the doctor and praised her for all she had done over the years. Her surgeon began to cry. Her doctors thought Michelle might survive another two weeks.

Chris left the hospital that evening to drive home and tell the girls about the seriousness of their mother's condition. It was the first time either parent had told the children how seriously ill their mother really was. "It was just so important to Michelle to protect the children as best she could from the nature of her illness," Chris said. "Nowhere in that whole time did she ever let them know that it was going to take her life." So Chris put both the girls to bed in Courtney's pink bedroom. "I just told them that we couldn't let her suffer anymore," he said. When they finally slept, he drove the thirty-five miles back to the hospital.

As Michelle lay in her hospital bed, an array of tubes and wires binding her to a battery of machines, Chris stood by her side and held her hand. Just that day, Chris told Michelle, one of his coworkers who attended a Pentecostal church sent him a couple of prayer cloths anointed with holy oil by his pastor and prayed over by members of his congregation. He showed them to Michelle, and with her permission he laid them on her bare stomach. Together they prayed for God's healing. It was Friday, August 3, and it was their sixteenth wedding anniversary. They still had each other and they still had hope.

The next morning, Chris brought the girls to the hospital to say goodbye. Together, the three of them stood by Michelle's bedside and prayed. "We told her that it was okay if she went to heaven," Chris said. "We weren't going to be selfish anymore." When Pati came in to see her, Michelle said to her sister, "Please let the girls know how much I love them, and how much I fought to be with them. Don't let them forget me."

A few hours later, Michelle's breathing evened out. Within an hour, she died, going peacefully with no coma, no seizure, no gasping for breath. A widely attended memorial gathering was held for her in Christ the King's gymnasium. The walls were dominated by a banner painted by Courtney in bright red poster paints: *My Mommy is in Heaven*. Later, the children released helium balloons into the blue sky. As the colored circles traveled higher and higher, Courtney turned to Patty Kalass and said, "My Mommy is up there catching them."

At the memorial gathering, friends and family were asked to write their favorite memories of Michelle on small cards that would be placed in a memory book to give Chris, Kaitlin, and Courtney. Many of the memories attest to Michelle's strong faith and how it inspired those around her. "Michelle didn't just talk about her faith, she lived it," wrote Jadi Meyer, a friend. "I called to cheer her up and she would lift me up by telling me how blessed she was with a loving husband and two precious girls. And how God had blessed her with such loving and caring friends. . . . She was a genuine, caring child of God." Marlene Frazier wrote, "What will I remember about Michelle? Although small in stature, she was strong in heart, love, courage, and faith. What a gift from God to have known her." And from Kelly and Rod Luetzen: "A true blessing. Be still and listen, she will speak to your heart."

Since Michelle's death, those who knew and loved her have tried to let her speak to their hearts, as they confront the questions that arise whenever a loved one dies. Why did Michelle have to go? Why didn't God heal her? Each of her friends and family has looked to Michelle's strong faith to bolster their own belief as they try to find answers to what are, ultimately, unanswerable questions.

Young mothers like Patty Kalass and Terry Magnani cannot help but ask, what was God's purpose in taking their friend away from her family? "I have asked, 'God, why, if Michelle had to work so hard to have these two girls, would you then take her away from them?'" Patty said. "But I believe that God has a plan for each and every person, and I believe that what happened to Michelle was part of God's plan. It is hard, but I am trying to look at it as God has blessed Chris with these two beautiful girls, and they will heal him and, as a family unit, they will survive."

Terry is more ambivalent. "I go back and forth between being angry that Michelle is without her girls," she said. "But at the same time, I am saying thank God for the girls now, because without them Chris would be a lost soul. And I think that is where the faith kicks in. How could we take another step every day if we didn't have this faith?"

Beth sees Michelle as an example for her own faith, and said she has learned a lot from witnessing her friend's passing. "If you have God as your basis, which both Chris and Michelle did, look at what you can accomplish, what you can survive," she said. "God doesn't just let these things happen to you. He helps you deal with them. That is something that I learned from Michelle."

Naomi Powell said that watching the grace with which her daughter handled her difficulties taught her a very powerful lesson. "In the beginning I was angry," she said. "I said to God, 'How could you do this to my daughter? Why?' But Michelle always said God has a master plan. And maybe that is what I learned from her, because I am not angry now. There is some sort of a peace inside me. I don't know what it is or where it comes from. But maybe I learned from my daughter that being mad at God gains me nothing."

"I don't think we are supposed to understand everything," Michelle's sister, Pati, said. "I just look at it as we don't know why. For me, it is almost the lesser of two evils: Either I accept God's will or I fight it, and there is no sense in fighting it. Obviously, I want her here, and I never wanted her to go through any of the suffering. But what is the point of arguing against God's will? But I guess that I just have to have faith. I don't understand it, but I know there is a purpose to it."

Polly Phillips also believes there is a purpose behind Michelle's death, though she is no closer to understanding that purpose after having watched her die. Still, Michelle's story has brought Polly a deeper understanding of who God is and how he works. "He is a loving God," she said. "Because even with the pain Michelle went through, he filled her and Chris with love and compassion. And where did that strength come from, if not from God?" Jean Potter, too, sees God's presence, and not his absence, in Michelle's fate. "Hope. That was what sustained Michelle over all those years," Jean said. "Maybe that was God's way of answering all those prayers."

Pastor Doyle Theimer prayed long and hard for Michelle to be healed, and yet she was not. In fact, he said, he has prayed for scores of people to be healed since he became a minister eleven years ago, and none of them has ultimately overcome their illness. But that doesn't deter him from believing God does heal, and when he does, that healing is "a concrete expression of his love," he said. But why didn't God show that kind of love for Michelle? After a long pause, he said, "God invites us to ask for healing. That's all we can do. We can't make him heal anyone. And I think the bottom line, as far as God's love goes, is that it has already been demonstrated on the cross. Every time I do a funeral, I am reminded that that is what it is all about—that our faith isn't just for this life. It is ultimately about our eternal life and our relationship with God." Michelle, he said, seemed to have understood that.

Her story, Pastor Doyle believes, teaches us not about the limits of God, but about the limits of this world. "Death is a reality," he said, his voice breaking over the words. "That is the hard part. But the real God is the one who has a good beyond that, and can bring good into it, and even a blessing out of it. And I think we see those blessings in hindsight. As a congregation, we just have to walk with Chris and the girls until they get far enough that they can look back on all this and find the blessings."

Maybe part of God's blessings—his "tender mercies" described in the psalm read at Michelle's healing service—is that in telling Michelle's story, other people will be touched and will find their faith strengthened. That, Pastor Doyle said, could be the real miracle of Michelle's ordeal.

Perhaps it is Chris who is left with the most questions. Why did God take Michelle away from him and her two girls? Why did she have to suffer? But even in the terrible, quiet echo of those questions, he has no doubt that God exists, and that he is a good and loving God who kept Michelle close to his heart. "Absolutely," he said unhesitatingly, when he was asked if he still believed in God. "But there is no good reason why Michelle is not here today. It doesn't make sense. I don't understand it, but it hasn't shunned me away from God, from Jesus on the cross."

In the weeks immediately after Michelle's death, Chris spent some time thinking about what he wants Kaitlin and Courtney to know and remember about their mother. At the top of his list is that their mother loved them, and fought as hard and as long as she did so she could be with them. "Her fight was about our family," Chris said. And he also wants them to know about her faith. "We need to make sure they know that their mother's faith was undying. We need to make sure they know that we will all be reunited again."

F O U R

Fondest Hopes
and Expectations

The Psychology Behind Belief
in Faith Healing

In 1818, a New England farmer named William Miller sat down with his Bible and calculated the Second Coming of Jesus Christ, based on a single verse in the Book of Daniel. "Unto two thousand and three hundred days; then shall the sanctuary be cleansed," Miller read in Daniel 8:14. The sanctuary, he believed, represented the world, which would be cleansed by the fires of the Apocalypse. Allowing each "day" to stand for a year, and reasoning the prophecy was made in 457 B.C., Miller reckoned that the end of the world would occur in or about 1843.

For twenty years, Miller worked and reworked his figures, and each time he came up with the year 1843. For twenty years he spoke of his beliefs to friends, neighbors, and, finally, to large gatherings of interested lay people and ministers. By 1842, the Millerites, as Miller's followers were called, published their own newspapers trumpeting Miller's predictions in several major cities—New York, Philadelphia, and Boston among them.

By that same year, there were tens of thousands of people who, like Miller, expected to see Christ's return in the year 1843.

The year 1843 came and went, and Jesus did not appear. For various reasons, some Millerites had pinned their hopes on April 23, 1843, while others awaited the end of the year. But with no sightings of the Seven Horsemen of the Apocalypse by December 31, Miller's followers were still not dissuaded from their beliefs. After each disappointment, they simply revised them. Sometime before the beginning of 1843, Miller restated his prophecy to say that he believed Christ would come according to the Jewish calendar, which would put his arrival sometime between March 21, 1843, and March 21, 1844. So as the end of 1843 passed, the Millerites told their many detractors, there was still time.

On March 21, 1844, the last day within the framework of Miller's revised prediction, the sun rose and set as usual. Again the Millerites were disappointed. But instead of considering that they might be mistaken, they again revised their prophecy and set about preaching it with even greater conviction. Judgment Day would occur seven months hence, on October 22, 1844. As the revised predicted day approached, Miller's followers became even more emphatic about the prophecy. More and more people packed into Millerite camp and hall meetings, farmers let their fields go unplanted, people sold their belongings and gave their money away. There would be no need of food and money in the new heaven, new earth, they reasoned.

Again, the much-hoped-for day came and went. But this time, after having been proven wrong three, even four times (depending on which dates each Millerite had pinned his or her hopes on), Miller's followers finally came to a general acceptance of the fallacy of their prophecy. The twenty-five-year-old movement disbanded virtually overnight.[1]

Why should it have taken so much to prove to so many that their beliefs were misplaced? Why did so many people want to believe in what most would deem a highly unlikely occurrence?

In the mid-1950s, a sociologist named Leon Festinger came across another religious band who fervently believed in the unlikely prophecy of a Kansas housewife. Mrs. Marian Keech claimed that "Guardians" from the planet Clarion had studied the earth and predicted that a devastating flood would sink the Americas from the Arctic Circle to Chile. The date of the flood, Mrs. Keech predicted, would be December 21, 1955. Like the Millerites, the group was disappointed. Also like the Millerites, they reexamined their beliefs and restated them in the context of their disappointment, devised explanations, and returned to their beliefs recharged.

Festinger wrote about this UFO cult in *When Prophecy Fails*, a 1956 work in which he and two coauthors theorized that believers in disproven religious hope, like a date-specific, apocalyptic prophecy, experience what Festinger called "cognitive dissonance." Basically, Festinger said, when people hold a belief that is dissonant, or incompatible, with what they see (some proof or action, like the sun rising on the Millerites after their much-anticipated dates) they are more likely to devise an explanation that will make that belief more consonant, or compatible, with what they see, than to abandon the belief outright.

Festinger's theory helps explain why some people will maintain the belief that God—and only God—will heal them, even as they remain sick, and in some instances, stare down their own deaths. But can we explain how the people described in this book are able to maintain their belief in a good, just, and loving God who takes a personal interest in their welfare, even when the circumstances of their lives seem to suggest that he does not? Why do people believe in what they cannot prove?

Dr. Margaret Paloma, a professor emeritus of sociology at Akron University, has studied faith healing in her own Pentecostal tradition. She says belief in it is experiential, not rational—people believe in faith healing not because to do so is reasonable, but because they believe they or someone they know has experienced it. As part of her research, Paloma has interviewed thousands of Christians about why they believe in faith healing, but one young woman stands out in her memory. The woman, a college student from a Pentecostal background in rural Kentucky, told Paloma of a woman she knew who had been in a wheelchair all her life. One day during a healing service at their church, this woman stood up and walked and proclaimed to all that God had healed her. The student told Paloma, "I respect my professors, but all I can say is, I know what I know what I know." That kind of experiential foundation is really the basis for all forms of religious belief, Paloma adds. "I don't believe [in God] because I read a book, I believe because I had an experience of God, and that made it real to me," she said. "I think Keirkegaard was right. There is a chasm between reasoning and faith." The leap, when it is made, is seldom an intellectual one, but an experiential one.

One could say the woman in the wheelchair was lucky. She asked God to act directly in her life, and believes her prayers were answered. But how do people who are not so lucky remain steadfast in their belief that God is not only good, but that he wants them to be healed?

William D. Dinges, a professor of religious studies at the Catholic University of America, says Judeo-Christianity is founded on the belief that God is a benign force—an idea that is hard to give up. "We do not start with the idea of a 'good God' and a 'bad God,' so we are compelled to maintain a kind of moral integrity for the divine," Dinges said. "Therefore, God can't ever be morally culpable. We have to find some other rationale" for why bad things happen. And if a person cannot find that rationale, the alternative is difficult, if not impossible, for most people to accept—that God is uncaring, unfeeling, and random in his works.

The inability to accept that idea of God is one reason many people disappointed in their hope for a faith healing will look for explanations. Dr. Nancy Hardesty, a professor of religion and philosophy at Clemson University who is currently writing about faith healing, says some people will decide their suffering is part of a divine plan, while others will blame themselves, or the sick person, for having some "secret sin" in their lives. "They explain it to themselves in a way that allows them to maintain faith in God's plan or God's sovereignty," she said. "But we don't know why, in religious terms, some people experience miracles and others, seemingly equally as devout, do not. And I think that is the hardest question for religious people: Why doesn't God answer prayer, or why doesn't he answer it the way we want him to?"

And that begs the question that most religions, at their heart, attempt to answer: Why does God permit suffering? Why does he allow illness and death? In the words of Rabbi Harold Kushner, why does God let bad things happen to good people?

Kushner set out to answer that in his 1981 best-selling book that took the question as its title. Kushner struggled with the question himself, when his young son, Aaron, died of progeria, an incurable condition that causes rapid aging. Even as he prayed for his son's life, as he simultaneously watched him die, Kushner was unable to give up the idea that God not only loved Aaron, but did not want him—or any other sick person—to die. "I believe in God," Kushner writes. "But I do not believe the same things about

Him that I did years ago, when I was growing up or when I was a theological student. I recognize His limitations. He is limited in what he can do by laws of nature and by the evolution of human nature and human moral freedom. I no longer hold God responsible for illnesses, accidents, and natural disasters, because I realize that I gain little and I lose so much when I blame God for those things. I can worship a God who hates suffering but cannot eliminate it, more easily than I can worship a God who chooses to make children suffer and die, for whatever exalted reason. Some years ago, when the 'death of God theology' was a fad, I remember seeing a bumper sticker that read, 'My God is not dead; sorry about yours.' I guess my bumper sticker reads, 'My God is not cruel; sorry about yours.'"[2]

Kushner argues that if God is limited in his actions, he is not limited in his compassion. And that is where true healing starts. Kushner warns that the seriously ill must make a distinction between asking God to "cure" them and asking God to "heal" them. And that, he holds, may require a total shift in the way one thinks of God, moving from the idea of an all-powerful being who can bestow or withhold his care, to an all-loving being who will endow the power to cope. "Sometimes we don't notice the miracle we actually get," he said in an interview. "We may ask God to take the tumor away, but the actual miracle may be that we get the resources to live with that tumor."

Maybe that is the kind of miracle Michelle Potter received— one that enabled her to maintain faith in a loving God who did not bring about the physical healing she and her family and friends hoped for. Maybe that is the kind of miracle that helped turn Mary Elizabeth Turk away from total faith in Robert Tilton, and back to the God she had known all her life. Maybe that is the kind of miracle that helped many of the people described here keep their faith in a God who did not always answer their prayers for restoration in the way they initially hoped.

And perhaps that was the kind of miracle the Millerites ultimately received. Though it was quite a different one from what they were seeking, many of them did, after their final disappointment, maintain their belief in God. The Seventh-day Adventist Church—today more than nine million members strong—was formed out of the ashes of the Millerites' final disappointment.

That disappointment was as bitter as that of anyone written about in this book. One of Miller's followers wrote after the day dawned on October 23, 1844:

> Our fondest hopes and expectations were blasted, and such a spirit of weeping came over us as I never experienced before. It seemed that the loss of all earthly friends could have been no comparison. We wept, and wept, til the day dawn. I mused in my own heart, saying, My advent experience has been the richest and brightest of all my Christian experience. If this had proved a failure, what was the rest of my Christian experience worth? Has the Bible proved a failure? Is there no God, no heaven, no golden home city, no paradise? Is all this but a cunningly devised fable? Is there no reality to our fondest hope and expectation of these things? And thus we had something to grieve and weep over, if all our fond hopes were lost. And as I said, we wept til the day dawn.[3]

Still, the day did dawn.

FIVE

It Is Better to Ask the Questions Than to Have All the Answers

Faith Healing and Traditional Medicine

Science and religion have long been on opposite sides of a seemingly bridgeless divide. Think of Galileo trying to convince the Catholic Church that the earth revolves around the sun, and not the other way around. But in recent years, especially in the last decade, medical science and religion have edged closer toward a mutual understanding and respect.

By Galileo's time, the church's influence in secular matters was far-reaching. Disease, both physical and mental, was generally thought of as affliction by evil spirits or demons. In the 1400s, most doctors were also Catholic priests or monks, but the church was clear about which discipline should be given the lion's share of their energies—edicts declared the clergy should focus more on ecclesiastic matters and leave medicine to the laity. The effect was to weaken the influence of religion on the practice of medicine.

By the twentieth century, the rift was deep indeed; and the value of religion to science was hotly debated, at least within the scientific community. In 1930, Sigmund Freud, a physician who became the father of psychotherapy, wrote that religious belief leads to "depressing the value of life and distorting the picture of the real world in a delusional manner—which presupposes an intimidation of intelligence."[1] Three years later, Carl Jung, also an early explorer of the human psyche, wrote that "losing a religious outlook on life"[2] could harm a person's mental health. And in 1941, the physicist Albert Einstein would comment, "Science without religion is lame. Religion without science is blind."[3]

After World War II, a number of scientists began a closer examination of the relationship between religious belief and mental and physical health. But, as scientific studies of religion continued to be generally frowned upon by the scientific community, their numbers were small and their studies were, too. But by the 1960s, the tide of thought began to turn slightly, at first perhaps, partly in response to a general awakening of Western cultures to Eastern thought, religion, and medicine.

Among the first to establish a link between a person's belief system and his or her health was Dr. Herbert Benson. In his 1975 best seller, *The Relaxation Response*, and in *The Mind/Body Effect* published four years later, Benson described how a state of deep rest achieved through a simple form of meditation could trigger the body's natural healing mechanisms. In a series of studies begun at Harvard University in the 1960s, Dr. Benson discovered that people with high blood pressure could reduce their heart rate, blood pressure, and overall anxiety by closing their eyes and concentrating on a single, soothing thought. Dr. Benson's work showed that when relaxed in this way, many patients could reverse their heart disease, and generally improve their health and well-being. To elicit the relaxation response, Dr. Benson suggested his patients repeat a word, sound, phrase, or prayer, such as "one peace," "the Lord is my shepherd," or "shalom." Largely as a result of Dr. Benson's work, Harvard established the Mind/Body Medical Institute in 1988, and both the Institute and Dr. Benson have furthered his original work. He is currently engaged in a multi-year study on intercessory prayer involving hundreds of patients.

Another pioneer in investigating the relationship between medicine and spirituality is Dr. Harold Koenig, director of the Center for Religion/Spirituality and Health at Duke University. In his book *The Healing Power of Faith*, Dr. Koenig describes how, when he was starting his medical career in the 1980s, he felt drawn to investigate the link he saw in many of his patients between religious faith and good health. When he announced his intention to devote his medical career to investigating a possible connection between the two fields, friends and coworkers were horrified, and tried to steer him away from what was at the time viewed as suitable only for the shady realm of televangelists. But Dr. Koenig, who describes himself as a devout Christian and a medical scientist, was not to be deterred. He and his colleagues at Duke have been involved in more than fifty studies that indicate a link between faith and health. Among their findings:

- People who attend church, pray, and read the Bible have lower blood pressure than those who do not.
- People who attend church regularly are hospitalized less frequently than those who do not.
- People who describe themselves as having a strong faith and who suffer serious illnesses have significantly better health outcomes than nonreligious people.

- People who attend religious services regularly have stronger immune systems than those who do not.
- Religious people tend to live longer.

Though the work performed at Harvard and Duke is widely respected, there are still critics, especially within the medical community. They point out that religious people may have better health because they are less likely to smoke, drink, or engage in other unhealthy habits, and that through their religious organizations, they tend to have broad networks of friends to care for them. There is also the placebo effect—the idea that people who believe they are receiving some sort of wonder drug (or form of faith healing, like intercessory prayer) will heal better and faster, even though the treatment is impotent.

Despite the controversy, medical professionals are increasingly recognizing the potential of their patients' belief systems as a means for healing. In 1996, the American Association for the Advancement of Science announced that, after reviewing 212 studies, three-fourths of them showed that a person's religious commitment had a positive effect on their health, especially with depression, addiction, high blood pressure, and heart disease. In 1997, the National Institute for Healthcare Research was founded with its primary focus on the intersection of faith and medicine. One of its first acts was to give money to eight medical schools to study how social and religious factors influence mental and physical health. Even more telling, at the end of the twentieth century, more than half of the nation's 125 accredited medical schools reported that they provide some kind of training in religion and spirituality for their students, up from only three schools in 1993, and the demand for such training is on the rise. Harvard Medical School's Department of Continuing Education routinely attracts as many as 600 doctors, nurses, social workers, and psychologists to its regional three-day conferences on spirituality and healing in medicine.

At Dallas's Parkland Hospital, Dr. Ron Anderson, the facility's chief executive officer, says he instructs his medical students always to consider a patient's faith. "If someone has a deep religious belief, that is a coping mechanism, and it may enable them to be ready to die," should it come to that, he said. "You never want to assault their belief system when they need it the most." Still, Dr. Anderson admits, a lot of research remains to be done to establish fully a faith-health connection. "At least it is a start," he said. "A lot of times it is better to ask the questions than have all the answers."

Dr. Richard P. Sloan of Columbia University's College of Physicians and Surgeons has many questions and concerns as to how doctors deal with their patients' religious beliefs. Dr. Sloan coauthored an article in the *New England Journal of Medicine* in which he questions the studies that link religion to better health, and takes healthcare professionals to task for generally being too eager to embrace religion as a form of treatment. The studies that support a link between faith and healing, Dr. Sloan writes, rely on "evidence [that] is generally weak and unconvincing, since it is based on studies with serious methodological flaws, conflicting findings, and data that lack clarity and specificity."[4]

He believes there are serious ethical considerations, too. In his paper, cosigned by a list of clergy, including a Jewish rabbi, a Muslim imam, a Catholic priest, and a Protestant minister, he worries that if doctors say religious practice has positive health benefits, they may also imply the opposite—that lack of religious beliefs leads to poor health. "Imagine that you pray and you go to church, and you hear this is good for your health, but then you get sick," Dr. Sloan said. "What do you say to yourself? Do you say I am sick because I haven't been sufficiently devout? I haven't been a good enough Christian? It is bad enough to be sick, it is worse to be seriously ill, but to add to that the burden of guilt and remorse for some supposed religious failure is unconscionable." Dr. Sloan has seen this guilt and blame in some of his own patients. He remembers sitting with a young woman awaiting the results of a biopsy for cancer. Sharing the room with his patient was another young woman who was also awaiting a cancer biopsy. When that young woman's results came back negative for cancer, her father, waiting with her, exclaimed, "We deserve this because we are good people." "What was my patient to think when her results came back positive?" Dr. Sloan asked. "That she was sick because she was a bad person?"

As a remedy, Dr. Sloan suggests medical professionals simply leave all questions of religion alone. They have neither the time nor the expertise to address them properly, he says. "Doctors would not expect an intern without cardiac training to do a cardiac catheterization," he said. "They should refer patients to professionals—in this case, professional clergy." Many doctors, it seems, are doing just that. In a 1998 survey published in the *Archives of Family Medicine*, the American Academy of Family Physicians found that 80 percent of its members refer patients to clergy and pastoral care.

Even medical professionals like Dr. Koenig and Dr. Anderson, who describe themselves as religious, say a person's faith is most beneficial as part of a battery of ways to combat sickness. They suggest that it isn't as important that a doctor believes in God's power to heal, as it is that his or her patient believes in it. Still, Dr. Koenig has written that a patient's all-or-nothing belief in faith healing can be a form of "negative religious coping" in that it can set them up for a terrible disappointment. But, if a sick person maintains a belief in God's power and ability to heal them in a variety of ways—physically, emotionally and spiritually—they are less likely to be disappointed. In *The Healing Power of Faith*, Dr. Koenig writes:

> I recognize that research can neither prove nor disprove the reality of answered prayers or divine intercession. By definition, a supernatural event is beyond the reach of scientific investigation. And I also accept that my role as a physician and medical researcher is different from the clergy's. But, although scientists cannot demonstrate whether God exists and intervenes in people's lives, I have learned that we can certainly explore and chart in a scientific manner the effect of religious faith and practice on physical and emotional health.[5]

There is at least one study that shows that too much reliance on faith healing can have tragic consequences. In 1998, Dr. Seth Asser of the University of California, and Rita Swan of Children's Healthcare is a Legal Duty (CHILD Inc.), published the results of their examination of the records of 172 children who died when their parents chose to bypass medical treatment and rely exclusively on faith healing. The majority of the deaths, this study concluded, were caused by conditions ranging from dehydration to diabetes, that could have been prevented if the children had received standard medical care—insulin injections, antibiotics, or removal of an appendix. Although there has been debate over the appropriateness of the methodology, Dr. Asser and Rita Swan found that, among the 172 children, 140 would have had a 90 percent or better chance of survival if they had received medical care.

Some of those in the CHILD study were from Christian Scientist families. While a number of sects and churches set a heavy emphasis on healing, the Christian Science Church, with more than 200,000 members at last report, is the largest in the world that promotes nearly complete reliance on divine healing. In publications such as *The Christian Science Journal* and *The Christian Science Sentinel*, church members have claimed that, in the church's 122-year history, there have been more than 60,000 successful healings resulting solely from prayer. Uncounted others rise to tell congregations of their healings at regular Wednesday night church meetings. But just as not every medical patient is healed by doctors, not every Christian Scientist has found that kind of healing through their beliefs. Marie Duncan was one of those who did not.

§ S I X

Earthquake

The Story of Marie Duncan

On Wednesday, February 28, 2001, an earthquake measuring 6.8 on the Richter scale rumbled its way beneath the Seattle–Tacoma area like a giant earthworm turning in the soil. The quake blew out the windows of the observation tower at the Sea-Tac airport, cracked the pillars of the state house in Olympia, crumbled some historic exteriors, and generally rattled people's nerves. But for Marie Duncan,* sitting in her small, two-bedroom apartment northeast of Lake Washington, it was nothing like the personal earthquake she experienced halfway across the country, in suburban Michigan, in the fall of 1974.

Marie, then twenty-four, was visiting the Christian Science church where she had grown up, not long after admitting to herself that she had not received the divine healing she had sought for her badly injured right knee. In the wake of that realization, she had allowed doctors to perform surgery on her—something strongly discouraged by Christian Science, which teaches reliance only on healing through prayer. Marie had every reason to expect that her return to church, made on a pair of crutches, would be less than warm.

---

* For reasons of privacy, the names of people and places have been changed.

But after the service, in which the church's First Reader recited, as he did every Sunday, from the writings of Christian Science founder Mary Baker Eddy, several Christian Scientists whom Marie had known and revered all her life as pinnacles of faith, came quietly to tell her not to be too hard on herself. They had had surgery and consulted doctors, too.

"That was an earthquake," Marie said at the memory, her cornflower blue eyes shining beneath a short bob of hair so blonde it is almost white. "That was a big one." And with it came an aftershock of realization for Marie. After a lifetime in the Christian Science church, she found herself asking, "What good is this CS?" she said, referring, as many former members do, to Christian Science by its initials. "It didn't heal my family's relationship problems. And I wasn't physically healed. Forget CS."

That was twenty-seven years ago. Now, at fifty-one, Marie said Christian Science still maintains a kind of hold on her, in that talking about it and thinking about it makes her angry. And it is understandable. Marie's decision to leave Christian Science has cost her dearly. Becoming free from the "tangled web of Christian Science," as Marie calls it, has affected her career, her friendships, her relationships with her family, her finances, and, most irretrievable, her health.

In the struggle to break free of what she sees as Christian Science's stranglehold on her mind and body, she has, at various times, turned to drugs, sex, and alcohol. More than once, she has been desperate enough to think of suicide. She has twice been in a mental institution. She has willingly sought counseling, more than once. Yet, throughout her ordeal, she has somehow been able to maintain the belief that, even though Christian Science is, as she calls it, "a lie," there must be some overarching truth out there, and it must be found in God. Yet even knowing that, has she, at different times throughout her life, struggled with anger towards God? She practically whispers, "Oh, yeah."

Marie was born in 1949, in Detroit, Michigan, the middle child and only girl in a family of three children. Her mother converted to Christian Science in about 1943, after going to a CS church with a neighbor. Marie's father came home from World War II to find a wife whose new religion held that all the horror he had seen as a soldier was merely an illusion, not real. It was the beginning of a rift between them that only grew wider through Marie's childhood.

Marie remembered, as a girl, attending a First Church of Christ, Scientist and sitting in Sunday school listening to the teacher describe how Mary Baker Eddy taught that all matter is an illusion, and that the real man is only an idea, not a physical being. That tree outside? That is an illusion. That chair she is sitting on? An illusion, too. The Christian Scientist must think only on God, or Spirit, and how she is a "perfect reflection" of him.

When she was a child, Marie asked questions, lots of questions. Where does evil come from? What is truth? How can the things I can touch and see, like this kitchen table, this chair, be illusions? And that got her in trouble, both in Sunday school and at home. Her mother would become enraged at her questions, telling her to raise her thinking above this supposed human reality, above being "merely human," Marie remembered. "There was this constant grind where you had to be perfect," Marie said, balling both hands into fists at the memory. "Mary Baker Eddy said I had to be perfect, and that I had to raise my thinking above being human. I have been striving to be perfect all my life, and I was always in a state of failure and guilt and shame. It was a terrible circle."

So, for the most part, Marie held her tongue and stuffed her questions and the growing pain inside. She went away to college at Western Michigan University in Kalamazoo to study to become a teacher. It was 1969, but for Marie, it was no Summer of Love. She was the victim of date rape. Devastated, Marie returned home for the summer. "When I told my mother about the rape, her response was that I was trash, that I was no good, and that it was too late for me," Marie said. "I felt worthless, a failure, a loser. Then, to add to all the shame I felt, I knew that according to Christian Science, my thoughts had opened the door and had allowed the rape to happen to me. The rape entirely was my fault."

In the summer of 1970, she began taking what Christian Scientists call "Class Instruction," a two-week intensive course in the teachings of Mrs. Eddy. In her book *God's Perfect Child*, former Christian Scientist Caroline Fraser describes what the students are taught:

> The "Primary Class" was a two-week, twelve-lesson course consisting of instruction in how to heal the sick and be[come] a practitioner. . . . Although class instruction is based, according to Eddy's rule, on the twenty-four questions and answers in "Recapitulation"—the chapter in *Science and Health* in which Eddy defines God, man, error, and other crucial concepts—students are nonetheless taught intriguing lessons that seem to fall outside the literal language of the chapter. These lessons derive from Eddy's own teachings. Students are urged to begin each day of their lives with a study of the Bible lesson for the week and of the "scientific statement of being" in order to protect themselves and their families against the threat of misfortune, illness, accident, or "aggressive mental suggestion," images of materiality presented by the outside world. In addition, they are taught a form of preventative, protective prayer in which

they "deny" the reality of evil in its most dangerous, specific forms: mesmerism, hypnotism, numerology, and other dangerous black arts.[1]

Among her photos, Marie keeps a class picture snapped after she and the twenty or so other adults—all middle-aged, except for Marie—completed the course. In it, the teacher stands before the class, a gray-haired woman smiling above a string of pearls. Marie stands to her left, with a big smile and her hands clasped demurely in front of her, the picture of Christian Science serenity.

But inside, she was in turmoil. She was learning that Christian Science teaching was true—absolutely—but that "truth" didn't seem to match up with her own life experiences. "I was one of my teacher's star pupils," she said, looking at the photo. "I thought that I would become a practitioner, and my teacher thought so, too." But she was still troubled by feelings of guilt and shame, both about her rape and about her belief in Christian Science. She felt in conflict. On the one hand, Christian Science teaching was that she was "perfect," but on the other, she felt unable to live out a "perfect" existence. "Intellectually, I 'got it,' but deep down, I didn't. People looked at me like I was spiritually elite, but deep down inside, I knew I was not. It created a deeper fear in me—that I had to protect myself from being found out as a fraud and a failure."

To calm the turmoil, Marie began drinking, not heavily at first, but soon, more and more. She also began taking up adventurous pursuits, like motorcycle racing and skydiving. One summer, she participated in the historical re-creation of a wagon train, traveling with other people, young and old, in nineteenth-century calico clothes and sunbonnets, making their rambling way across North Dakota in a line of horse-drawn covered wagons.

It was on one of these wagons that Marie had a serious Christian Science crisis. On one segment of the trip, as they were riding slowly across North Dakota, it began to rain so heavily that everything—people, horses and wagons were soaked through. Marie was up front with the driver. When she stepped down by placing a foot on the spokes of a front wheel, she slipped and fell, and heard something crack. It was her right knee. Her companions picked her up, wrapped her rapidly swelling knee for the night, and packed her into the back of the wagon. In the morning, her knee was so enlarged that the bandages had to be cut off. The decision was made that Marie could not continue on the wagon train and should be taken to a doctor in Jamestown, the nearest town.

But Christian Scientists do not go to doctors, Marie explained to one of the leaders of the wagon train. Christian Scientists do not believe in illness, or disease, or suffering. These things are only illusions. Christian Scientists can cure themselves and others through prayer, and that was what she was going to do.

And why not? It was no less than what Mary Baker Eddy, the founder of Christian Science, trumpeted that she had done. Born in 1821 in Bow, New Hampshire, Mrs. Eddy was repeatedly plagued with mysterious ailments. She tried many popular remedies of the day, both medicinal and folk, but until she was forty-five years old she was almost never well.

Then, in 1862, she heard of a mesmerist, or hypnotist, named Phineas Parkhurst Quimby, who claimed he could cure disease and illness. Mrs. Eddy immediately went to see him, and almost as immediately, saw the bulk of her symptoms disappear. She submitted herself to his care and teaching, and soon became his most avid student.

Four years later, Quimby died, and two weeks after that Mrs. Eddy slipped on a frozen sidewalk and fell. Confined to her bed, Christian Science legend has it that she asked for her Bible and read a passage—she never told which one—in which Christ heals the sick. It was then, she later said and wrote, that the "biblical Truth" in the form of the doctrine of Christian Science was divinely imparted to her. She reportedly left her bed and walked. For the next nine years, she wrote and rewrote this doctrine into what would eventually become *Science and Health With Key to the Scriptures*. Originally published in 1875, Mrs. Eddy revised it more than four hundred times before her death in 1910, at the age of eighty-nine.

Truth, as Mary Baker Eddy saw it, is that all matter is false and does not exist. Only Spirit, or God—whom Scientists also call Principle, Mind, Soul, Life, Truth, and Love—is real, and man is his perfect reflection. According to Mrs. Eddy, a Christian Scientist is already unified with God, since he is a perfect reflection of God. A Christian Scientist's goal is to understand fully this true relationship to God. A key way of understanding this truth is by repeating "the scientific statement of being," composed by Mrs. Eddy: "There is no life, truth, intelligence, nor substance in matter. All is infinite Mind and its infinite manifestation, for God is All-in-all. Spirit is immortal truth; matter is mortal error. Spirit is the real and eternal; matter is unreal and temporal. Spirit is God, and man is his image and likeness. Therefore man is not material; he is spiritual." If a Christian Scientist correctly understands the scientific statement of being, he will experience no disease, illness, suffering or pain.

For two weeks, Marie lay in a bed in Jamestown and tried to get her mind over the matter of her broken knee. She read her copy of *Science and Health*. She repeated the scientific statement of being over and over. She prayed, trying to heal herself as she had been taught in Christian Science; her prayer and thoughts running something like this:

"I know that God created me in his image and likeness. I am spiritual, good, and perfect. Mortal mind tells me I have a mortal body that can be injured and have pain. But I know that a mortal body is a false representation of man. Since sin, disease, and death are not real, I have no mortal body, no injury, no pain."

But, after two weeks of no healing, Marie felt like a total failure—a feeling that was becoming all too familiar for her. If only she could understand the "Truth" of Christian Science, her knee would be healed. This injury was her fault. She had only herself to blame. After two weeks of listening to her non-Christian Scientist friends telling her she must see a doctor, she finally gave in. "This was the ultimate failure," Marie said now. "I felt I was literally carrying a ton on my shoulders. I had done the unforgivable—I had had surgery."

After recuperating for a week in Fargo, North Dakota, Marie returned home to Detroit to live with her mother. Her mother was ashamed of her bandages and crutches and refused to take her to church. When Marie finally did return to church, she was confronted with the paradox of knowing that some of her fellow Christian Scientists, who had once seemed so pure in their belief in Mrs. Eddy's teachings, had, at times, relied on traditional medicine.

Meanwhile, Marie's personal and family problems were mounting. Her parents were separated and thinking of divorce after thirty-three years of marriage. The war in Vietnam and the Watergate cover-up had also deeply disappointed and angered her. The best way to get away from it all, Marie thought, was to leave. She signed up for the Peace Corps, and set off for Liberia in West Africa in December 1974. "I intended never to return to the U.S. or to my family," she said. "I hated them both."

For a while, everything went well in Liberia, at least on the surface. Marie was teaching, something she loved and found fulfilling. Her pictures from this time show her with a wide smile and bright blue eyes, clad in the colorful clothes Liberians love so much. In the pictures, her young students wear smiles almost as wide as their teacher's.

But presenting a perfect face to the world was something Marie learned from Christian Science. Inside, she felt a huge void. "I was a master at being two people," she said of this time. "I was very good at dressing nice and at being compassionate." But she had begun drinking again, this time heavily. She was promiscuous and considered returning to drugs. In her heart, she found she still believed Christian Science was "the Truth," but felt that because she could not live up to its demands of perfection, God could not possibly love her.

By March 1976, worn out from keeping her pain and confusion to herself, Marie became ill. As her Christian Science beliefs still held her, she tried once again to heal herself through prayers. Again, she failed, and again, she blamed her own spiritual poverty. As she had done after her failed attempt at healing her knee, she finally agreed to friends' requests that she see a doctor.

"[The doctor] asked me about my relationship with God," Marie remembered, which surprised her into frankness. "I said it was nonexistent. I didn't know where to start. I said I didn't know if God would forgive me." The doctor, an evangelical Christian, suggested that Marie meet and talk with his wife. Together, the two women prayed, and Marie was invited to spend the weekend and go to the local mission church with them.

At the church on the day Marie visited, the adult Sunday school was studying cults. The cult, as they defined it, for that day's session was Christian Science. Marie felt her face burn. She was already uncomfortable being with people she had been taught were spiritually inferior, as well as being in this church with its large cross—something never found in a Christian Science church, where *Science and Health* holds a place at the altar. Still, her curiosity got the better of her. She raised her hand and said she had been raised a Christian Scientist and could tell them anything they wanted to know about it. She ended up talking for an hour. At the end of the day, the doctor and his wife suggested she read some biblical passages about the need for salvation and the deity of Jesus, two doctrines Christian Scientists do not hold. Marie was touched at the welcome she felt from everyone at the church, said goodbye, and returned to her post upcountry.

It was a turning point for Marie. She stayed awake most of that night, comparing the Bible to the writings of Mrs. Eddy. "For the first time in my life I was willing to put CS on the line," Marie said. "I didn't know what was the truth, but I had to find it. I remember getting on my knees about four A.M. and saying to Jesus, 'You are God.' That is blasphemous in CS. From that day forward I never returned to CS. I became a born-again Christian. And life started to make sense."

A couple of weeks later, Marie was baptized in the lagoon behind the mission station, off the Pacific Ocean. Her new pastor waded with her into the cool water. A few yards out, they turned to face the 100 or so people gathered at the bank as witnesses. Marie spoke about how she had been raised in a cult, and she had now found the true path. Her pastor laid his hands on her forehead and back, and in one quick move, dipped her back into the water. "It was the most awesome experience for me," she said, now fingering a picture of herself waist-deep and wet in the light brown water. "My baptism was an outward illustration of what occurred in my heart. It demonstrated a new life. For me publicly to stand up and say Christian Science is not the truth, and that I have found the absolute truth in Jesus . . . that for me was quite emotional."

Marie may have left Christian Science, but Christian Science had not left her. For the next nine months, she remained teaching in Liberia and joined a small group of Christians, students, and missionaries, in study and prayer. But she was unable to shake the fears and self-doubt she had fallen into as a result of her failed Christian Science healings. And now she had even more questions about Christianity and about her new relationship with God, whom she had come to call her Lord. What is prayer? How does prayer in Christianity differ from prayer in Christian Science? What is sin? Is man born with a tendency to sin? Why is there evil in the world? What is true faith? And, what is the relationship between prayer, faith, and God's sovereignty with respect to healing?

When her time in the Peace Corps was up, Marie spent nine months in Europe before returning to the United States. After a brief, uncomfortable time at home with her disapproving mother, Marie left home again and eventually settled in Denver, Colorado. She began attending a Presbyterian church and started making friends. She liked the church and felt she was spiritually on the right path.

Then, in March 1979, she reinjured her right knee while playing a game of racquetball and had to be carried off the court. Doctors said she needed an ACL reconstruction—the rebuilding of the anterior cruciate ligament, one of the major support structures of the knee. With the return of her injury came the return of her self-doubts and her fears of being spiritually unworthy in the eyes of God. Just before the surgery, she sought help from a group within her church that practiced healing.

Eight or ten people gathered about Marie, who was seated on a chair in the middle of their circle. They all laid their hands on her, bowed their heads, and prayed aloud. If she had faith—the *right* kind of faith, *enough* faith, the leader implied, she would walk. When their prayers came to a close, they asked her to stand up and give it a try. "I couldn't walk," Marie said. "I got blamed again. I was told I didn't have enough faith." Only this time it wasn't the Christian Scientists who she felt were berating her; instead, it was the Christians. "All the guilt and shame and other feelings from CS were back, large and strong," Marie said. "When I explained to people at church what was happening, that I was caught again in CS thinking, they just told me, 'No, you are out of CS, you have a new theology, just have faith and believe. Just change your thinking.'" That last part—just change your thinking—was too close to Christian Science for Marie. She went ahead with the surgery.

After her surgery, Marie took a teaching position in a school a good distance from her church. Midway through the year, emotional pressures disabled her, and she resigned. She felt now she needed to return to Detroit and to try to reconnect with her family. "I still felt everything was my fault," Marie said. "I'm spiritually inferior. I'm no good."

Back in Detroit, Marie's parents had divorced, and her mother had remarried. Marie moved in with her mother and new stepfather, a man who had been one of her Christian Science Sunday school teachers and someone she dearly loved. She settled at another evangelical Presbyterian church and, while there, required another ACL reconstruction on her right knee. In

December 1981, Marie's father died. Always the closest to him, she was devastated. Her comfort was that shortly before his death, her father had become a Christian. Marie felt sure that, when she died, she would be reunited with him in heaven.

He had left her an inheritance, and she decided to use it to attend seminary in order to find the answers to her questions about God.

At seminary, Marie felt that she had finally found a safe place to ask all her questions. The seminary was evangelical and also ecumenical, offering teachers from backgrounds as diverse as Pentecostal and Anglican, but who held the same core beliefs about Christianity. But by her third year of study, Marie began to have doubts about what path she should take after seminary and to feel an acute sense of loneliness. She began to drink alone at night in her home. Again, she found herself embodying what she most hated about her Christian Science upbringing, a façade of serenity masking pain and anger.

When the drinking intensified to the point that she began to think of killing herself, she checked herself into a mental hospital. Some of her classmates came to visit her, and several felt moved to confide in her. They told her some of the horrible things they had endured and kept secret—drug addiction, child abuse, alcoholism. When Marie was released from the hospital, she felt confused about her fellow students' lack of transparency. "At seminary, it was safe to ask theological questions, but not safe to share who you are, your personal problems and hurts that needed help and healing," she said. "I left seminary in some ways healed, because many of my theological questions were answered. For example, I had really begun to comprehend that Jesus Christ is my Redeemer, and that the Bible alone is God's truth and doesn't need Mrs. Eddy's writings to interpret it. These were pivotal issues for me because of my Christian Science upbringing. But on the other hand, my relationship with the Lord shifted and changed, because of my disappointment in my fellow Christians."

After leaving seminary in 1985, Marie settled in Seattle, where she has lived ever since. But she could not shake the feeling that a real relationship with God had somehow eluded her. By day, she relied on Valium to get her through her new job at Boeing, where she had found work in computer technology support. At night she began drinking heavily, again alone and at home. For a while, she attended a charismatic Christian church, even turning up drunk for one Sunday service. Her pastor, a recovering alcoholic, confronted her, but she denied that she had a drinking problem. Later, alone in her home with a drink, she hit rock bottom and called him. She attended Alcoholics Anonymous the next day, March 26, 1987, her AA birthday and the last time she had a drink.

After eight days without a drink—eight difficult days during which she continued to work during the day and attend AA meetings at night—Marie decided she needed professional help to stay sober. A counselor at Boeing immediately found her a bed at an inpatient treatment center. But the more sober Marie became, the more rage surfaced. Rage at her mother, at Christian Science, at different churches she had attended, and "especially God," she said.

The treatment center relied on AA's "Twelve Steps," the third of which required Marie "to make a decision to turn my life over to God," she said. It was a stumbling block. "I couldn't and I wouldn't do the third step," she continued. "I didn't trust God and I blamed him for my upbringing and all the subsequent events in my life." Though the third step is a voluntary one, the center's counselors asked her to stay for an extra week, worried that if she skipped it she would drink again. At the end of the week, and after much internal struggling, Marie said she "finally felt the presence of God." She could trust, again, in his goodness. She left the treatment center and returned home.

Marie's struggles for sobriety and for faith began to take a toll on her health. First she had a stroke, from which she has completely recovered. Then she suffered a neck and back injury that put her out of work for ten months and has left permanent damage. In 1993, through some volunteer work she was doing with recent Russian immigrants, she contracted tuberculosis.

The last straw came in July 1992. Marie slipped and fell on her kitchen floor, crashing down onto her left knee, the one she had not hurt before. Marie found herself flat on her back, staring at the ceiling, unable to get up. "The experience triggered memories of my being raped," she said. She felt completely alone, completely forgotten by God. Something inside her snapped. "It was as if my rape had just happened," she said. "I just felt totally helpless, as if it were happening again. And I just went into a rage. More than ever, I just wanted to die. I lay there and said, 'I hate you, God. I hate me. I hate my family.'"

A few days later, Marie took a medical leave from Boeing and checked herself in to a Christian counseling clinic in the Seattle area. She felt she was right back where she had started twenty-three years earlier—before leaving Christian Science, before becoming a born-again Christian, before joining AA.

But the clinic's doctors were sensitive to her anger at men and at God and to her background in CS. At the suggestion of her therapist, she went to a nondenominational, evangelical Christian church, which she continues to attend. There she met the Rev. Terry Brandon, her current pastor, who, Marie said, has personally nurtured her through her recovery, both physical and spiritual.

Rev. Brandon describes Marie's struggle with her faith as similar to those of other people he has known who have suffered what he describes as "long-term mental abuse." He likens the kind of self-dependence on faith healing that she had been taught in Christian Science to a "form of brainwashing." Those who try to break away from such a background face, what he calls, "a long journey with many false starts." By sharing his own grief over the death of his daughter who died suddenly at the age of twenty-five, Rev. Brandon has tried to help Marie see, in the very essence of her physical and spiritual pain, a powerful example of God at work in her life. "If my personal hope were only in this life, none of this suffering would make sense," he said. "But I step back from it and realize this life is a crucible in which we learn some value of eternity. When I look at Marie's life, I don't see only the struggle and the pain. That would be discouraging, whether it was Marie's or anyone else. But the fact that she is living and breathing and sitting in my office today shows that there is some healing, that there is a supernatural presence that has saved her and brings all of the rest of this together. There is an eternity she understands out of her pain more than she did before. I understand eternity in much deeper terms today because of my daughter's death. That is not excusing the pain; it is coming to a deeper understanding of it."

Rev. Brandon supported Marie's wish to enter a nonprofit residential facility for cult rehabilitation. With the help of its counselors, she was finally able to understand what she sees as the stranglehold Christian Science had on her mind and her feelings. When she left, she felt freer of its grasp than ever before. She has also joined a support group for former Christian Scientists that meets periodically.

Marie's relationship with God is on the mend, but her body is not. In September 1995, she returned to work at Boeing, only to have her department downsized and to be laid-off herself within the year. She tried a number of full-time and part-time jobs, but her arthritis and fibromyalgia had begun to aggravate her extensively. In the last three years, she has been diagnosed with pernicious anemia, which causes painful neuropathy in her feet and legs, and with some kind of autoimmune disease which her doctors are still unable to diagnose. She also required surgery on her left shoulder and a total replacement of her right knee. In the spring of 2000, she had to quit work entirely. In late 2001, she had a total knee replacement on her left knee. She has run through her savings and is now living on disability benefits. She cannot walk without the use of a cane.

But what she can do is read her Bible every day. And, for the first time in her life, Marie says she knows in her heart that it holds that absolute truth she has always sought. "That truth is the bedrock of my faith," she said. "The Bible helps me to finally feel the Lord's love and to accept my physical limitations without feelings of spiritual failure. My hope extends beyond this life—I have a sense of eternity."

She has also come to a clearer personal understanding of what she sees as the relationship between faith and healing. Healing is not something to be received as a reward for the right understanding, the right prayers, good works, or a donation to a glossy pompadoured televangelist. It is a gift of God's grace. "I have the same objections to faith healing as I do to Christian Science healing," Marie said. "There is this works mentality—that if you pray hard enough, if you have enough faith, you will be healed. That's just not what I see when I read about people of faith in the Bible. Salvation is a free gift, based on faith and not performance. But when you ask for physical healing, you may not receive it. God sometimes say 'no' to physical healing, even when your faith is strong."

There are still some things she doesn't grasp. She doesn't yet fully understand Bible passages that describe God as "protector." "People say to me that God has protected them from so many things. And I say, oh yeah? Well, it sure doesn't feel like he has protected me. Yet when I remember past traumas in my life, I can see specific instances where he unquestionably carried me through the difficulties. So I may not completely understand how he is my protector, but I accept it as true, because it is in the Bible. I know ultimately my answers are in Jesus and in the Bible."

When she is feeling especially purposeless, or at the mercy of an uncaring universe, she turns to the principles found in 2 Corinthians 8:11–12 (NIV): "Now finish the work so that your eager willingness to do it may be matched by your completion of it, according to your means. For if the willingness is there, the gift is acceptable according to what one has, not according to what he does not have."

"God is not asking me to be Billy Graham," she said after reading this passage aloud. "He is asking me to do the best I can. Just do according to what you have. And that is such a peace."

She has sometimes felt that God has used her best to benefit others in different ways. Once, Marie was moved to join a healing circle at her church and to lay her own hands on the broken knee of a fellow church member. As she prayed for God to heal the woman, Marie felt something move under her hands. The woman, previously in great pain, was able to get up and walk.

How does Marie explain why God would use her as the instrument of someone else's healing, even as he withholds her own? How can she still believe in his goodness?

"That is the big question," she says. "Why does God choose to heal some and not others? That is still very hard for me to understand. I keep asking, 'Why do you answer my prayers for other people, and you don't answer my prayers for me?' I don't get an answer. Sometimes that makes me feel depressed and very low, and sometimes I can just let it go. It is all part of learning to live with God's silences."

When she feels God's silence, she turns to Hebrews, chapter 11, her favorite in the whole Bible. It is her favorite because it is a Christian hall of fame, beginning with Abel, murdered by his brother, and ending with the prophets, who were tortured, flogged, stoned, jeered at, sawed in half, imprisoned, impaled, and otherwise persecuted, all for their faith in God. At the chapter's end, she reads, "These were all commended for their faith, yet none of them received what had been promised" (v. 39 NIV).

"I love this chapter," she says, looking up from her Bible. "A lot of these people didn't receive many of the things they were promised. But they understood that, like God's promise of the coming Messiah, not all of his promises would be fulfilled within their lifetime. God commended them for their faith—faith that he would fulfill those promises according to his timetable, not theirs. To me, that is the final refute to all those faith healers who would say you don't have enough faith, or you remain sick because you have sin in your life. The Lord asks us, in the midst of our doubt, pain, anger, and fear, to trust him and him alone. Hebrews 11 says, 'Faith is being sure of what we hope for and certain of what we do not see.' My hope is in eternity with the Lord, and I'm becoming even more certain of God's faithfulness. This is what the ancients were commended for. They had more faith and more trust in God than other people, and God commended them for their faith."

Is she a member of this hall of fame?

"I don't know," she says after a pause. "That's up to the Lord. But I think maybe anyone with faith in Jesus Christ is a member."

In His Plan

The Story of Debbie Shepherd

Debbie Shepherd was eight years old when she came to her mommy and said her tummy and her back hurt.

Her mommy, Linda Shepherd, figured her daughter had a kidney infection. Linda had once been sick with the same ailment, so she told her daughter to do what she had done—drink lots of water. That way, Linda explained to the girl, she would have to go to the bathroom and then she would feel better. For the next three months, whenever Debbie often stopped playing or eating or doing her homework to tell her mommy about her aching tummy and back, Linda was worried but chose to trust God. God would heal Debbie, just as he had healed so many members of her family before.

Then Debbie—usually bright and active—stopped eating. She got thinner and thinner, and then her stomach seemed to get bigger, even though she ate little. One day, while helping her daughter change clothes, Linda discovered a golf ball-sized lump in her daughter's abdomen. It was time to do something.

But Linda Shepherd and her husband, Bob, both now in their fifties, did not believe in taking their eleven children to the doctor.

They were members of a small, fundamentalist Christian church with fewer than twenty families, though their pastor had followers scattered throughout the world. Together, they shunned the outside, material world in favor of what they saw as a richer, more spiritual one.

So Bob and Linda did not consider taking Debbie to the local hospital. Instead, they felt they should take her to see their minister, who would pray over her and ask God to heal her.

That decision may have cost them their daughter's life. When her distraught parents finally did bring her to a doctor, Debbie Shepherd was diagnosed as having a Wilm's tumor, a form of childhood kidney cancer that is among the most treatable if caught early. Debbie's was not. Yet throughout her illness, which lasted more than a year, Debbie's ordeal brought her stricken parents to a deeper knowledge of who God is and how he works in the world and in his children's lives. But the cost of that knowledge was high—too high. Debbie Shepherd lies buried near Brandy Creek in the mountains above Redding, California.

Bob and Linda laid Debbie to rest eighteen years ago, but that was not the end of their trial. In the intervening time, both Bob and Linda have managed to put aside much of their anger—at themselves, at their minister, and at God—and much of their grief. Still, they bear the bruises and scars of people who have been through great misfortune. In place of their anger, Bob explained, is a new realization of who God is and what trust in him really means.

"After Debbie died, that broke down some walls for us," Bob said, wiping his eyes on a napkin at a fast-food outlet in Redding's heart. "It opened us up to new opportunities, to new people. I would never wish that tragedy on anyone, but some good things came out of it." After another moment, he added, "Time heals."

Linda had been born in a Navy hospital in Oakland, California, in 1950. Not long after her birth, her father, a former Navy seaman, moved Linda and her mother to Minnesota, where, at a prayer meeting, he felt a call from God to preach. Linda says her family never stayed in one place for long, because her father's "itchy feet" had taken them from one place to another— Washington, Minnesota, Iowa, and a handful of towns dotting the plains of Kansas.

So much moving around made a lonely, isolated life for Linda, the eldest child in a family of seven boys and three girls. She would just make friends at one school when her father would announce that they would be packing up and moving across the state or across the country. When Linda finished the eighth grade, her mother told her she wanted to go back to work, so Linda would need to stay home from school to take care of the children and the house. Linda got through the ninth grade by correspondence.

After a year, she was allowed to return to school, this time to high school in Topeka. Before long, the family moved again, this time to Salina, Kansas, where Linda graduated from high school in 1968. She then went to live with her grandparents in Arizona. Three months after her arrival, her parents came to pick her up, their bags and belonging all packed, and announced the whole family would now be moving to Fresno, where their church, Christ's Church of Restitution, was relocating.

Christ's Church of Restitution was like so many other small, independent full-gospel churches of the 1960s, that evolved out of the Pentecostal revival of the early 1900s. It was driven by an energetic pastor called Brother Bee.* Brother Bee had a gift for preaching, marked by a powerful and charismatic way of speaking that often evoked a deep emotional response in his followers. He had survived the Depression, World War II, his sister's suicide, the death of his father, and his mother's fatal illness. "He had a sureness and a hardness which I found intimidating," Bob said. "Yet it was not spiritual arrogance that came across as much as experience, too much experience. And I never felt arrogance in his personality; it was more the ups and downs of life he had been through." Sometimes, Brother Bee reminded Bob of the prophets in the Old Testament—full of passion and conviction and a deep reverence for God. He was well versed in Scripture and could quote the King James Bible front to back. Like many Pentecostal preachers, Brother Bee taught full reliance on God and the Bible. "He had an impressive command of Scripture," Bob said. "His citing of the verses came seamlessly, and they were always germane, always apropos. . . . He was a very thoughtful, very perceptive person."

Brother Bee warned his followers to be wary of worldly people and things. They were to be "in the world, but not of the world," Bob said. For this teaching, Brother Bee had to look no further than his Bible for an array of Old Testament warnings against the things of man. Among those most often quoted was Jeremiah 17:5–8, "Cursed be the man that trusteth in man, and maketh flesh his arm, and whose heart departeth from the LORD. For he shall be like the heath in the desert, and shall not see when good cometh; but shall inhabit the parched places in the wilderness, in a salt land and not inhabited. Blessed is the man that trusteth in the LORD, and whose hope the LORD is. For he shall be as a tree planted by the waters, and that spreadeth out her roots by the

* The man called Brother Bee here died several years ago. Since he could not be interviewed, out of fairness he has been given a pseudonym

river, and shall not see when heat cometh, but her leaf shall be green. . . ."

One way Brother Bee interpreted this passage was as an admonition against doctors and medicine. It was an interpretation, like so many of his teachings that had come out of his own painful experience. When his mother was ill, doctors were unable to help her, and, he seemed to feel, may have made her worse in the long run. So, if someone was sick, it was Brother Bee who would lay hands upon them, anointing them with the Lord's ability to heal the afflicted and the wounded. Bob and Linda believed he had a true gift for healing.

One night, not long after making the move to Fresno, Linda and her family attended a prayer meeting at a church member's home. There, in the center of the room, was a stranger, a young man over whom everyone was praying. He had long, curly dark brown hair, auburn eyes, and a light, almost sallow skin. The moment Linda set eyes on him, she knew God intended her as his "helpmeet."

If Linda's early life was peripatetic, Bob's was more rooted. He was born and raised in Fresno, in the heart of California's vast, flat breadbasket, the Central Valley. After finishing high school in the late 1960s, he went to Fresno State University to study English. A lot was going on in California in the 1960s. Vietnam protesters came to the Central Valley, together with rock and roll, folk music, and drugs. Bob was involved in all those things. "I was at a loss as to the direction of my life and felt I was adrift," he said. "I was sort of into trying anything, trying everything, but mostly it was pot, or inexpensive wine. Ultimately, a crisis came. I was desperate. With a nudge from my dad, I got help through a detox program at Fresno Community Hospital." It was during this time that he met Linda at the prayer meeting.

In 1970, one year and eight months later, the couple was married in Christ's Church of Restitution, with Brother Bee both officiating and giving the bride away. Almost immediately, they started a family, with Linda staying home and Bob working as a gas station attendant. Later, he would hold a number of other jobs, including factory worker, landscaper, and ranch hand. The children—all eleven of them—were born at home with a family or church member acting as midwife. Linda would have nothing to do with hospitals or doctors, because she was taught to "trust in God," she said. At each birth, Bob was there by his wife's side to receive the baby as it emerged. If Linda had a difficult delivery, they would call Brother Bee to pray for her. During her labor, Bob would sometimes read the Bible aloud to her. Their first child, Isaac, was born at 4:18 in the morning. The time seemed portentous; when they called Brother Bee to announce Isaac's arrival, he suggested they read the corresponding verse from the Gospel according to Luke: "The Spirit of the Lord is upon me, because he hath anointed me to preach the gospel to the poor, he hath sent me to heal the brokenhearted, to preach deliverance to the captives, and recovering of sight to the blind, to set at liberty them that are bruised." The verses were, Bob said, a kind of commission, a calling from the Lord. Thereafter, the Bible provided the names of most of the children: after Isaac came Naomi, then Deborah Elizabeth Shepherd, born on January 19, 1974, then Benjamin, Ruth, Esther, Matthew, Rachel, Martha, Charles, and Abigail.

In the early 1970s, Brother Bee told the church elders that he had "a leading" to move Christ's Church of Restitution farther north to Lewiston, California, a small town in the mountains west of Redding. Some families decided to move north with the church, and Bob and Linda soon followed. In 1980, they settled about an hour and a half away from the church in Redding, a city which is guarded by Mount Shasta to the north, Mount Lassen to the east, and the Trinity Mountains to the west. Spreading south, like the train of a wedding dress, is the long, low flatland of California's Central Valley.

In 1982, Debbie became sick. When her parents discovered her tumor, they called Brother Bee. The minister, who had known Debbie since her birth, asked that the girl be brought to the church's grounds in Lewiston. Bob called his mother, Jean, and asked if she could accompany them on the trip and stay with Debbie if Brother Bee needed her to remain in his care for a while. They all set off on the trip through the mountains in Jean's new Volkswagen Rabbit.

Debbie and her grandmother stayed with Brother Bee for a week. In accordance with James 5, he prayed the prayer of faith over her, laying his hands upon her and anointing her with oil. Still, she did not improve. At the end of the week, Brother Bee asked Jean to take the girl home. Jean drove Debbie down out of the mountains and returned her to Bob and Linda, telling them that Brother Bee said Debbie had "decided to die."

Bob and Linda were stunned. They believed God to be all-powerful, ever-faithful, and quick to reward the just; and, as members of Brother's Bee church, they were certainly among the just. It simply was not within their scope of belief to think that he would fail to heal their beautiful child, and the shock began to crack the certainty of their faith.

"It was like BOOM, it just hit us horribly," Bob said. "We just didn't believe that we would lose Debbie. We saw only that God can do all things. We knew a host of Scriptures along those lines. There was a flaw there. There were things that were wrong, but we blinded ourselves."

When Debbie returned to her parents, Brother Bee advised Bob and Linda to take her to the local hospital. It would, he explained, be a protective move for them if anyone accused them of neglecting their daughter. So Bob and Linda put Debbie in their car and drove the couple of miles to Shasta General Hospital's emergency room.

Walking through the hospital's double doors was difficult for the couple. They were taking their daughter out of the arms of their minister, a man they had trusted fully for years, and were handing her over to doctors and nurses, people they had been taught to distrust. But they also felt they were being obedient to God's will and honest about their belief in total reliance on Him.

When Shasta General's doctors saw Debbie, they wanted to admit her for tests. She was weak, pale, and had a lump on the side of her abdomen. But Bob and Linda said they wanted to take her home. They explained that they were Christians who believed only God, not man, could heal their child. To give Debbie any kind of medical treatment would be against their religious convictions. To their surprise, the hospital staff said they understood. They said they knew Bob and Linda had a right to believe what they wanted and had no intention of trying to sway them. But they also wanted Bob and Linda to understand that it was their belief that they could help Debbie, and that they had a duty to try and do so by reporting them to the local child protection agency. Bob and Linda said if that was what had to be done, then that was what had to be done. In the meantime, Bob and Linda said, they wanted to take their daughter home.

After Debbie was settled in her bed, Bob and Linda went to Child Protective Services themselves. They explained to the social workers there about Debbie's illness and their beliefs. Again, they expected to face people they had been taught were "ungodly," "worldly," or, at best, "lukewarm Christians." Again, they were surprised by the kindness they met.

"There were so many people who were kind to us," Bob said of that day. "People we thought were the enemy were so respectful of us and of our beliefs. They were almost apologetic."

Child Protection Services agents explained that the state of California would have to file in state court for medical custody of Debbie, which would allow them to seek medical treatment on her behalf. But they also explained they understood Bob and Linda's predicament and would ask the judge to allow Debbie to remain at home during her treatment. Bob and Linda, stunned by the kindness they were receiving, assented, and later a judge granted the request.

Debbie was taken from Redding to Sacramento, about 165 miles to the south, to the hospital at the University of California for the bulk of her treatment. She had chemotherapy, radiation, and surgery to remove one of her kidneys. After the surgery, Linda asked to see her daughter's kidney—a request that previously would have been unthinkable to her. "The kidney was double its size and black and gray colored," she remembered. "That made it real. That made it human. It was as if I needed that proof to make it real to me."

While Debbie lay in her hospital bed, her parents remained angry and confused about their daughter's illness. Bob, especially, acted out his pain. At the hospital, he was hostile towards doctors and nurses, as if they were the cause of all Debbie's trouble. Yet, again, he was surprised at the kindness and consideration he received at the hands of those he had once thoroughly ignored and despised. "I was not a very cooperative parent," he said. "My attitude was that these guys were the enemy. But somehow I think they knew that we were reacting out of pain at watching our daughter die. They were so kind to us, and now I am so grateful."

Dr. Charles Abildgaard, a pediatric hematologist and oncologist, spearheaded Debbie's medical team. Even after almost twenty years, he remembers Bob. "He was difficult," Dr. Abildgaard said. "And I remember a little girl who was badly malnourished and wasted." He also remembers Debbie's Wilm's tumor as one of the largest he has ever seen, perhaps the size of a softball. "It was really a bad situation," he said.

Just before Debbie's surgery, Dr. Abildgaard asked Bob if he and Linda would agree to the doctors resorting to "heroic measures" to save her life, if the situation came to that. Bob remembers that he waffled. "I just could not hear the words 'end of life issues,'" he said. "I just could not stop believing that God was going to save our little girl, so why were we even talking about heroic measures?" Even though the state had control of Debbie's healthcare, Dr. Abildgaard still patiently laid out the choices for the anguished couple. He knew Debbie was still their daughter, no matter whose care she was in, and, out respect for them, he treated Bob and Linda as if the choice was still theirs to make. Bob and Linda left it up to the doctors to do everything medically possible to save their daughter.

It was an exchange that slowly began to turn Bob's heart and shake all he had previously held as gospel truth. Some of the very people that he and Linda had thought of as uncaring or unChristian seemed to embody the very essence of Christian caring and compassion. They wanted to fight for his daughter's life as much as he and Linda did. "The people we thought were our enemies turned out to help us more than our friends," he said.

Dr. Abildgaard said neither he nor the other hospital staff had any special religious sensitivity training at the time Debbie was their patient. In deciding how to deal with Bob and Linda's religious beliefs, he simply relied on his humanity. "I don't think it matters whether you are dealing with someone's religious belief or with some other deeply held conviction, I think you have to handle it the same way," he said. "You have to be honest with them, listen to them, explain things to them, but draw the line about what is the best thing for the child. You have to do what you think is right."

Debbie remained in the hospital for two months. At Thanksgiving, the whole family drove down to Sacramento to be with her. Later, they learned that when they left, she had cried inconsolably for days. When nurses later reported this to Bob and Linda, it broke their hearts. They missed their little girl. They were thrilled when, at Christmas, doctors pronounced Debbie well enough to return to Redding. They prescribed more chemotherapy, which could be performed in a hospital not far from her home.

For the next eleven months, Debbie had chemotherapy at Redding's Shasta General Hospital. For a time, she was well enough to return to the homeschool she had attended, which was run by members of the church. But because she was undergoing medical treatment, which church members opposed, some of them made her feel unwelcome. Linda remembers children making fun of her daughter and recalls a time when a teacher snatched the wig off Debbie's bald head, because, she said, it was "a vanity."

There was anger and frustration at home, too. How, Linda and Bob asked themselves, could they explain to the rest of their children that the God they had taught them to expect would heal the sick—especially the righteous—would not heal their sister? "They would ask questions, and we would say we didn't want to talk about it," Linda said. "But I could see it was hurting them."

Eventually, Debbie again became too ill to go to school, so Bob and Linda set her up in an old brown vinyl recliner they had in their living room. Linda was pregnant again, and when the time came to deliver baby Charlie, Debbie lay beside Linda, wiping her forehead with a damp washcloth. Two weeks later on November 5, 1983, Debbie Shepherd died at home. She was nine years old.

After Debbie was gone, Bob and Linda and their children gradually stopped making the trip to the church in Lewiston. Brother Bee and his wife, Sister Mary, told them Debbie's death was not their fault, and that they should never blame themselves, but Bob and Linda could not seem to accept that in their hearts. Neither, apparently, could some of the other church members. At times, Bob and Debbie felt unwelcome. Some church members advised them "to forget about Debbie and move on," Linda said. Others simply refused to acknowledge their loss. In the end, they felt judged by the very people they hoped would embrace them in their grief. "We felt condemned," Bob said. "They didn't have time for our pain."

At the same time, Bob and Linda wrestled with their belief in God. Bob went through a period of rebellion against God, along with a great deal of anger. "I went through a time when I blamed everyone. I blamed Brother Bee, all religious people, God. I blamed anyone I could, because I had made up my mind that no one was going to take my little girl from me. No one." He was also angry with himself for ignoring the blind spot in the faith he and Linda had ascribed to. It wasn't that they had misplaced their faith in God; he, they came to realize, was still the same loving being they had always known. But they had also come to know that their previous conception of God failed to see his presence within suffering and loss. "Where we were blind was in limiting God to our own demands and expectations," Bob said. "God was there all along. We just didn't see him. He was in the people we thought were our enemies. He was in that sickness we thought was the enemy. . . . If God is only God of life—and nothing more—I think that is not enough."

They also learned a number of things about themselves. Bob feels he has become less judgmental of other people. "We were not the first to have experienced loss or pain," Bob said. "I think, in some way, our faith was untested. . . . Losing Debbie gave me a humanity. I am a fellow sufferer. I am down here," he said, placing his left palm about waist level. Then he raised his palm above his head. "I am no longer on this level up here." Linda said she learned that she is strong and that she can "trust the Father." But it was also a lesson in learning to trust others. "It is okay to ask for help when it is needed," she said. "He does use people to help those who need it." And she says that even when it seemed God was not there, he was. "God the Father goes with us through the garden," she said. "Just like the song says, 'I go with you, with you, all the way.'"

Although their daughter died, Bob and Linda do not feel they failed her. Instead, they feel they did the best they could for her with the ideals and values they had then. "I feel like we didn't fail Debbie, because we took her to the Lord for him to do with her what he would," Linda says. "Then we went the next step," turning her over to doctors. "Everything was according to his purpose and to his plan. And Debbie never blamed us. She knew the Lord would heal her if it was in his plan."

For a time after Debbie's death, the Shepherds didn't go to any church at all. Then they visited one here, one there, but could not find a place where they were comfortable. Everywhere they went, they felt they heard a strain of the isolationist teachings, the messages of spiritual superiority, which reminded them of

Brother Bee. Now they attend an independent Baptist church in the Redding area.

A couple of years ago, on the advice of a friend, Bob and Linda created their own Web pages. In different ways, their internet sites have served as an outlet for their grief and a place where they can each explore their new understanding of God. Linda's site* reads like a story book, filled with memories of meeting and marrying Bob, about the births of her children, and of her sadness at the loss of Debbie. Bob's site** is titled "A Family's Grief and Guilt." Beneath a tiny picture of Debbie's smiling face is the subtitle, "Where were you, Lord?" The text reads like the journal of someone trying to work through a deep anguish, someone who wants to warn others against making a similar mistake. At the end, Bob spells out what he has come to believe after Debbie's death:

> We learned other things, too. Like how important it is to be gentle . . . That God can meet you in many forms and that he can use many agents and channels for his blessing. No longer are we impressed with the logic of distrusting all doctors and all government. Indeed, even if there is truth in the scriptures which say we must not trust in man, we know God does use human intermediaries.
>
> Yes, people, tell your churches. Tell your friends. Even if God 'spanks' his people, even if we sometimes suffer affliction or sickness or loss, He has not abandoned us. And guess what!! God does use science for good. He does use doctors for good. He does use government for good.
>
> This insight was Debbie's gift to us. Thank you, Debbie. We love you.

* http://lindy1950.tripod.com
** wysiwyg://19/http://geocities.com/robbi01

EIGHT

God's Will Be Done?

Faith Healing and the Law

It would be wonderful to be able to write that Debbie Shepherd was the only child who was kept, at least initially, from traditional medical care because of her parents' religious beliefs. But, even as medicine and religion learn mutual respect for each other, scores of children have died—and continue to die—due to what many child advocates have come to see as religious medical neglect.

In Pennsylvania, at least nine children whose parents were members of Faith Tabernacle, a sect that favors faith healing over modern medicine, have died of treatable illnesses since 1983. One boy, a twenty-two-month-old hemophiliac whose condition went medically untreated, bled to death in 1997. Two of the children were from a single family: eight-year-old Clayton Nixon, who died of an ear infection, and his sixteen-year-old sister, Shannon Nixon, who succumbed to treatable diabetes while her family prayed and read the Bible over her. Her blood sugar level was eighteen times the normal level at the time of her death. Insulin would have saved her, just as simple antibiotics would have saved her brother.

In Colorado, an estimated thirty-five children whose parents were members of First Assembly and Church of the First Born, a faith-healing sect, were buried between 1974 and 2001. Eleven of those deaths occurred in the last ten years. Among the dead are Angela Sweet, a first-grader who died in 1990 of peritonitis caused by a ruptured appendix, and Warren Trevette Glory, aged eighteen days when he died of meningitis in 1999. Billy Ray Reed, also an infant, died from a common heart defect in July 2000. He was followed only a few days later by Ishmael Berger Belebbas, born dead after lying in his mother's birth canal for several days. Most recently, thirteen-year-old Amanda Bates died of complications of untreated diabetes, including gangrene. Medical professionals assert all probably would have survived with medical intervention.

One of the most recent and heinous cases occurred in Oregon City, a suburb of Portland. There, in June 1998, a state medical examiner became suspicious of a pine-dotted cemetery owned by the 1,200 members of the Followers of Christ Church, a Pentecostal sect that shuns doctors and medical treatment in favor of faith healing. They also bury their children at an alarming rate. An investigative series by *The Oregonian* newspaper showed that of the seventy-eight children buried in the graveyard over a period of thirty-five years, twenty-one would probably have survived with medical intervention. Among the dead is Alex Dale Morris, a four-year-old who contracted a fever in February 1989. Church members prayed over the child for forty-six days before he died at home. An autopsy showed one entire lung was filled with pus—an infection that could have been overcome with antibiotics. Another child, eleven-year-old Bo Phillips, died of treatable diabetes while more than one hundred church members were gathered in his home to pray for him. When local detectives found the child at his home, covered by a sheet, his father made a statement, later repeated by the church president—"God's will be done."[1]

But it is the First Church of Christ, Scientist, the largest faith-healing denomination in the world, that has been most plagued by scandals surrounding child deaths. The trouble started in 1902, when a young girl died of diphtheria after her Christian Science parents refused her diphtheria antitoxins, (then a new treatment for the disease). In 1937, a ten-year-old girl died in a diabetic coma when her Christian Science aunt denied her insulin. In 1956, a seven-year-old boy died of the same illness when his Christian Science parents withheld the same treatment. At first, these cases did not cause a widespread public outcry. They seemed like sad, isolated incidents caused by misguided parents, and they were not widely reported in the press or investigated by law enforcement officials. Then, in 1967, a flood of public sentiment broke out against Christian Science when a five-year-old Massachusetts girl died after contracting a strep throat. Her mother, a Christian Scientist, prayed over the girl for three weeks. She died in her bed of untreated pneumonia, and an autopsy revealed the child suffocated because her lungs were filled with pus. A month later, her mother, Dorothy Sheridan, was indicted for manslaughter. Prosecutors portrayed Sheridan as medically neglectful, while the church defended her rights to religious freedom and to choose alternative care for her daughter. Since 1967, the untimely deaths of Christian Science children have peppered the news headlines.

Among the dead are Robyn Twitchell, who was only two-and-a-half years old in 1986, when he died in Boston of peritonitis caused by a bowel obstruction. The boy was sick for five days, during which his parents consulted a Christian Science practitioner and a Christian Science "nurse," and prayed for him. The boy died in his father's lap, vomiting his own feces and bits of his own bowel.

Elizabeth Ashley King, a twelve-year-old Phoenix girl, was pulled out of school for what her parents explained was "a problem with her leg." The problem, discovered months later by a detective alerted by school officials and Child Protective Services, was a tumor on her right leg that measured forty-one inches in diameter. Under a court order, a doctor diagnosed the girl with bone cancer and estimated that she would have had up to a 60 percent chance of survival if she had been treated in time. Ashley's parents continued to deny her medical treatment and, instead, committed her to a Christian Science nursing home, where patients receive only nonmedical care. She died there in 1988, reportedly in great pain.

But perhaps the Christian Science child death case with the greatest fallout has been that of Matthew Swan. Matthew, born in Michigan in 1976, was the second child of Doug and Rita Swan, two devout and life-long Christian Scientists. Both had been teachers at Principia College, a Christian Science school, and both were "class taught" Christian Scientists, having completed two weeks of training in the church's theology and healing methods.

When Matthew was fifteen months old, he came down with a fever. A Christian Science practitioner had been successful in treating his previous ailments, so the Swans relied on a practitioner again. But this time, Matthew did not recover. Instead, he grew only worse. For almost two weeks, he lay on his bed, either motionless or suffering convulsions and screaming fits. For almost two weeks, his parents agonized between taking him to a doctor and relying on Christian Science. Finally, unable to bear Matthew's suffering any more, they rushed him to a hospital emergency room. Doctors told the Swans that Matthew had bacterial meningitis and required emergency neurosurgery. A week later, Matthew Swan died.

From the moment of Matthew's death, the Swans turned their back on Christian Science. In 1983, as a tribute to their son, they founded CHILD, Children's Healthcare Is a Legal Duty, a non-profit agency that seeks to protect children from religious medical neglect. Based in Iowa, where the Swans raised their two other children, CHILD, Inc. works to educate the public about religious groups that shun medical treatment for their children, and to change existing state and federal laws that they believe protect medically neglectful parents on grounds of religious freedom.

Currently, forty-one states have religious exemption statutes that shield parents from criminal prosecution, when their sick children perish while being treated exclusively with some form of faith healing. States which allow a religious defense of serious crimes against children include Iowa and Ohio, both of which allow religious defense of manslaughter; Arkansas, which permits religious defense of capital murder; and Delaware and West Virginia, which both permit religious defense of the murder of a child.

Ironically, it was just such a law that protected the Swans from prosecution in their own son's death—Michigan has a religious exemption law that shields parents who have sought religious treatment for their children. The origin of Michigan's law, and similar laws in most states, can be traced to the Christian Science Church. Beginning in the 1950s, the church began lobbying for protection of its practitioners, who have no medical training, and its nursing homes, which provide no medical care. The church held then, and continues to hold now, that its members are protected by the First Amendment's promise of freedom of religion. In 1955, as the United States Senate opened hearings on the freedom of religion, the church composed a long document describing the ways they felt their religious freedoms were being curtailed—everything from required vaccinations and inoculations, to compulsory medical examinations for federal employees, and fluoridation of water. Over the next several decades, the Christian Science Church successfully won for itself, and for members of other faith-healing sects, most of the exemptions it sought. They also persuaded the Internal Revenue Service and major insurance companies to count payments to Christian Science practitioners, nurses, and nursing homes as deductible medical expenses.

Then, in 1974, the federal government, again with lobbying from the Christian Science Church, made religious exemption laws a requirement for states seeking federal money for child abuse prevention and treatment programs. And while the federal government cancelled that requirement in 1983—after years of lobbying by CHILD and its supporters—the statutes have remained on the books in most states. Currently:

- 48 states permit religious exemptions from immunizations for children.
- 8 states allow religious exemptions from screening for lead poisoning.
- 6 states permit religious exemptions for students from instruction about disease and illness in school.
- 5 states permit religious exemptions from physical examinations for schoolchildren.
- 4 states allow religious exemptions from silver nitrate eye drops for children, which can prevent blindness in babies infected with venereal disease by their mothers.
- 4 states have a religious exemption from hearing tests for newborns.

- California has a religious exemption from tuberculosis testing for public school teachers.
- A majority of states permit religious exemptions from metabolic testing for newborns. These tests detect disorders that can lead to retardation and other handicaps if untreated.

Advocates for children have argued that all of these exemptions have eroded the rights of minors and they are working to have states repeal them.

Officials of the Christian Science Church hold that such religious exemption laws permit them to practice their faith as they wish. One Christian Science official said church members prefer the term "religious accommodation" over "religious exemption," because they do not want to be "exempted" from something, but want recognition of their right to choose alternative healthcare—in their case, a reliance on divine healing through prayer. "The reason people want these accommodations is so they can choose Christian Science care, which they consider better care," said Brian Talcott, the head of the Christian Science Church's Committee on Publication for Northern California. Rather than freedom of religion, Talcott said, "the issue is more the popular notion of what is good care, and that is changing. There is an assumption in our society that if you seek medical care, you've done the right thing. If you haven't, it's not the right thing. There needs to be a more balanced look at what is appropriate care, and parents need to make sure they are responsible in deciding what is appropriate care."

Talcott said there is no official Christian Science doctrine condemning members who resort to medical care, and that the church has recently moved to make its members more aware of that choice. In 1983, 1991, and 1999, the church's board of directors issued official statements on the matter. One statement, printed in the *New England Journal of Medicine*, reads in part, ". . . it is not to satisfy the requirements of a dogma or the dictates of a church that Christian Scientists rely on spiritual means for healing, both for themselves and their children. There are no such requirements and no such dictates." The statement goes on to say that if some members turn to medical treatment, "they are not—contrary to some recent charges—stigmatized by their church." When asked why, if this is so, there have been so many Christian Science child deaths, Talbott replied, "I don't understand that myself. It is not church teaching. It's how [the parents whose children died medically untreated understood Christian Science."

Tom Denison, a fifth-generation Christian Scientist and a Colorado attorney who has filed briefs on behalf of the church in his state, says the Christian Science Church in no way wants to protect anyone's right to abuse or neglect a child. "We don't feel anyone has a First Amendment right to deny effective care to their child," Mr. Denison said. "We are interested in preserving matters of choice."

At this time, CHILD notes that there are at least sixteen different religious groups that forego medical treatment for faith healing. Some of these groups are well-known and well-established, like the Christian Scientists. Others are smaller, more secretive sects, like Jesus Through Jon and Judy, the Believers Fellowship, Faith Assembly, the Source, and End Time Ministries. No one knows how many children, in these groups and others, die annually from religiously motivated medical neglect. Some of these faith-healing sects are close-knit and secretive. Most fail to report infant deaths to the authorities, and conduct burials themselves. The Followers of Christ were found to have buried numerous babies that were born and died at home, with no birth or death certificates to mark their passing. Others call county law enforcement and medical officials only after their children die. In 1998, Rita Swan and Dr. Seth Asser, then a critical-care pediatrician at Methodist Children's Hospital in San Antonio, Texas, published a paper in the professional journal *Pediatrics* that attempted to number these children's deaths. They analyzed 172 reported deaths of infants and children between 1975 and 1995, and found that 140 of those children would have had a survival rate of 90 percent or higher if they had received medical care. The children, from twenty-three different religious groups in thirty-four different states, succumbed to ailments including appendicitis, dehydration, labor complications, and vaccine-preventable disorders. One child, a two-year-old, choked on a banana while her terrified parents gathered church members to pray.

Yet very few of these parents are charged with a crime. In the case of the Followers of Christ, prosecutors found their hands tied because Oregon's religious exemption laws protect faith-healing parents from charges of murder by abuse, manslaughter, criminal mistreatment, and criminal nonsupport. In Colorado, charges of manslaughter and negligent homicide were dropped when the parents of Warren Trevette Glory, the eighteen-day-old child who died of meningitis, pled guilty to less serious charges of criminally negligent child abuse. They face no jail time, only probation.

But the lack of prosecution does not mean law enforcement officials are insensitive to the plight of these children. Oregon prosecutor Terry Gustafson spoke to *The Oregonian* about the death of eleven-year-old Bo Phillips from untreated juvenile diabetes, and of her decision not to prosecute his parents. "I want desperately to prosecute this case. I think that what happened to Bo Phillips is a horrible, horrible thing." But, as Gustafson found out in her own state, the current scramble of laws surrounding children and the religious beliefs of their parents makes it difficult for her to do her job.

Caroline Fraser, a former Christian Scientist who has written a critical examination of the church in her book *God's Perfect Child*, says the current jumble of laws places those entrusted with enforcing them in a tight spot. "I think this is where politicians, judges, and people who work for children's services are profoundly troubled and confused about what they should do," Fraser said, "because you have someone who is a loving and devoted parent, and yet they are doing something horrible to their child. Society has to step in, and yet sometimes it does not have the right to because of the ways the laws are currently written."

Even when convicted, parents in these cases don't always face the fullest penalties allowed under the law. The parents of Ashley King, the girl with the forty-one-inch tumor, pled guilty to felony child abuse, which was reduced to reckless endangerment, a misdemeanor, after they served three years probation. In 1995, an Oregon man who was a member of the Church of the First Born was charged with criminally negligent homicide in the death of his seven-year-old son from a treatable form of leukemia. The man was convicted by a jury and sentenced to probation by a judge. The Faith Tabernacle parents of Clayton Nixon, the eight-year-old who died of an ear infection, were sentenced to probation and community service. And when seven-year-old Amy Hermanson died of untreated diabetes in Pensacola in 1986, the Florida Supreme Court overturned her Christian Science parents' conviction for child abuse and third-degree murder. The judges found the state's religious exemption laws "too confusing" for the average person to understand, and therefore, obey. Similarly, when Laurie Walker of Sacramento, California, was convicted of manslaughter in the 1984 death of her five-year-old daughter from bacterial meningitis, a federal court overturned her conviction because, it said, California law did not provide fair notice of her liability, should her daughter die while undergoing Christian Science treatment, which provided only prayer for the girl. According to CHILD, there have been only thirty-seven convictions in cases of religious medical neglect of children since 1982.

The Supreme Court has refused to hear four cases of religious medical neglect since 1988. One of the most recent cases refused was that of Ian Lundman, an eleven-year-old Minnesota boy who lived with his father and died of treatable diabetes while visiting his Christian Science mother. Douglass Lundman, the boy's father and not a Christian Scientist, sued his ex-wife and several Christian Science practitioners and officials. A jury found the boy's mother, Kathleen McKown, her new husband, their Christian Science practitioner, a Christian Science nursing home, and a local church official jointly responsible for the boy's death. Mr. Lundman was awarded $5 million in compensatory damages, and the church was charged an additional $9 million in punitive damages. On appeal, Mr. Lundman's award was reduced to $1.5 million, and the Supreme Court refused to review the case.

But recent cases, like the one in Oregon, have prompted a wider, national movement to repeal religious exemption laws. The Academy of American Pediatrics, the American Medical Association, the National Committee for Prevention of Child Abuse, the United States Advisory Board on Child Abuse and Neglect, and the National District Attorneys Association have all spoken out against these laws. CHILD maintains a constant vigilance for cases of religious medical neglect of children, and has filed several lawsuits of its own together with numerous amici briefs. In one of those cases, Flores v. City of Boerne, the American Professional Society on the Abuse of Children joined

CHILD in arguing that the Religious Freedom Restoration Act compromised the ability of states to protect children. The Supreme Court ruled the RFRA unconstitutional in 1997.

Slowly, the laws are changing. In 1994, Minnesota passed a law requiring parents to notify child protective agents if they plan to forego medical treatment in favor of faith healing when their children are seriously ill. So far, no parent has reported under this law. In Oregon, the large number of graves cradling children from the Followers of Christ Church prompted local law enforcement officials to lobby state legislators to introduce a bill that would limit or eliminate religious exemption for parents with seriously ill children. In August 2000, Oregon governor John Kitzhaber signed into law a bill that repealed five religious exemptions which denied children medical care. Judges may now impose prison sentences on faith-healing parents convicted of second-degree manslaughter, criminal mistreatment, neglect, and criminal nonsupport.

But Oregon law continues to allow religious exemption in cases of murder and first-degree manslaughter, and also allows a religious defense to criminal mistreatment of fifteen- to seventeen-year-olds who hold their own religious beliefs against medical care. And in April 2001, Colorado governor Bill Owens signed a bill that repealed the state's law permitting parents a religious defense when their children die under faith-healing treatment. The new law no longer explicitly protects Christian Scientists, despite recognition of their treatments by Medicare and major insurance companies, but the real target was the First Assembly and Church of the First Born, with its cemetery full of children. Five other states—Hawaii, Massachusetts, Maryland, South Dakota and North Carolina—have also repealed their religious immunity laws on the grounds that the Fourteenth Amendment, which guarantees all citizens equal opportunity under the law, makes them illegal.

For Rita Swan and other members of CHILD, those changes are not enough. "I believe all religious exemptions from child health care laws are wrong, and I will continue to work for their repeal," Swan said in an e-mail interview. "Laws requiring therapeutic, preventative and diagnostic health care of children are enacted for the protection of children. Children should not be denied such care because of their parents' religious beliefs." Fraser agrees. "Society has an obligation to insure that the rights of these children are respected as much as the rights of the parents to their religious beliefs," she said. "The child's right to life trumps the parents' [right] to their beliefs."

Brian Talcott of the Christian Science Church also agrees that the state has a responsibility to see to the proper care of children. But he warns that portraying the situation as a case of the rights of the child versus the rights of the parents is an oversimplification. The crucial question, as he sees it, is whether or not the state can ensure that, when religious healing practices are involved, the children in question are being cared for responsibly. "Parents have the responsibility to provide good healthcare for their children, but that is not the issue here," he said. "In a society unused to viewing healthcare outside conventional medical practice, it is not surprising that some have challenged [the practice of] spiritual healing for children . . . [but] should families be limited to conventional medical methods for children when other methods with a positive track record are available to the public at large?" To Brian Talcott, and uncounted others, the right to alternative healing methods—faith-based or otherwise—is a fundamental right.

NINE

Rise Up With Healing

The Jewish Healing Movement

In 1987, Paul Cowan was a journalist for the *Village Voice*, and his wife, Rachel, was a student. Both were also observant Jews. Every morning, Paul strapped on phylacteries and prayed. Rachel, a convert from Unitarianism to Judaism, was studying to be a rabbi at New York's Hebrew Union College. Married for twenty-two years, the Cowans together had raised their children and had collaborated on a number of books.

One night in 1987, Paul suddenly became quite ill, running a consistent fever and complaining of aching joints and extreme tiredness. Rachel rushed him to the emergency room at New York Hospital. Lab tests came back indicating that he had an aggressive form of leukemia.

Rachel Cowan found herself in an unenviable position. At the time of Paul's diagnosis, she was studying grief counseling as part of her last year of rabbinical school. Now, her husband, Paul, would become the first person she would care for and counsel.

When Paul was in the hospital undergoing treatment, Rachel would sit in the hall outside reading from the book of Psalms. When he asked her to find a blessing for his radiation treatment, she found it in the last chapter of Malachi: "But for you who revere my name, the Sun of righteousness shall rise up with healing. . . ."

Paul Cowan died in 1988 during Rosh Hashanah, the Jewish New Year, a time in the Jewish calendar of spiritual renewal and rebirth. After her husband's death, Rachel Cowan worked through her grief in the only way she knew—within the Jewish liturgy and the Jewish Scriptures. Out of this process, she and a number of other young rabbis and laypeople helped develop what has now become known as the Jewish Healing Movement.

Thirteen years after Paul Cowan's death, the Jewish Healing Movement has spread from New York to San Francisco and to many places in between. There are now twenty Jewish healing centers nationally, and twenty other groups have shown a desire to start their own centers. The movement has made tentative progress in other countries, with congregations in England and France having expressed an interest in holding their own Jewish healing services, or in establishing their own Jewish healing centers. The centers offer healing ministries that are uniquely rooted in Judaism, to Jews of all backgrounds.

"Our perspective is one of many, but we are pretty straight in our perspective," said Susie Kessler, coordinator of the National Center for Jewish Healing in New York, a kind of headquarters for the movement. "We talk about healing, not in terms of a physical cure, but in terms of wholeness. Even healing into death is part of that concept. It is the concept of 'Shalom,'"—the Hebrew word for peace—"which is very big."

The philosophy underlying the Jewish Healing Movement is different from the healing movement in the Christian tradition, in that it focuses not so much on asking God for a cure, but in looking to the Jewish tradition for ways of coping with illness, both chronic and fatal. The term "faith healing" is not used in the Jewish tradition, although Jews do pray for God's divine healing. But more than physical healing, the Jewish Healing Movement strives for emotional healing and spiritual wholeness in the face of illness. Coping with grief, both that of the sufferer and his or her loved ones, is also a major focus. To help people understand this kind of suffering, the Jewish Healing Movement looks to established Jewish tradition—the liturgy, writings, prayers, customs and rituals of this 6,000-year-old religion with 14 million adherents worldwide. "We are interested in reconnecting people with the tradition they already have and know," said Kessler. "Someone once described it to me as 'coming home.'"

But from Paul Cowan's death to today's Jewish Healing Movement is a long, circuitous route. In 1989, the newly ordained and newly widowed Rabbi Rachel Cowan wanted to dedicate her pastoral career to helping the sick. Over the next few years, she and Nancy Flam, a former classmate and fellow new rabbi, discussed how their religion might better serve suffering Jews. Around 1991, they met with some similarly interested laypeople in a kind of informal think tank. Out of that meeting, and with the help of a three-year seed grant from the Nathan Cummings Foundation, the Bay Area Jewish Healing Center was established in San Francisco, while a national center was founded in New York City.

As the first of its kind, the Bay Area Jewish Healing Center established a number of programs focused on emotional and spiritual healing, including spiritual support groups for people with illnesses, a Jewish hospice, and Camp Tawonga, an annual summer gathering for the bereaved, both children and adults. In the last several years, its services have expanded to include support groups for people grieving the loss of a loved one, for those living with chronic illnesses, and for a time, for doctors caring for the terminally ill. Recently, it initiated a support group for caregivers, the spouses and partners of the chronically and terminally ill.

Phyllis Eisenman-Lampert is a member of this last group. Her husband, Herb Lampert, who is seventy-three, has frontal lobe dementia and recently had to move out of the couple's tri-level house in woody Mill Valley and into a nursing home in a nearby city. Every day, Phyllis, who is sixty-seven, spends four to six hours visiting him—talking to him, feeding him, tidying his room, and otherwise taking care of him. The spirit of community and caring she has found through the Bay Area Jewish Healing Center has been "the high point of my trip through Judaism," she said. "I think I have come from being very angry and resentful about my loss, to being very accepting and grateful for the time we have left. I see people differently. People are just doing the best they can, and Herb is just doing the best he can."

Rabbi Natan Fenner is the spiritual leader of Phyllis's support group, and shares its direction with a therapist. Formed in February 2001, it was a response to the isolation its members— all women in a single congregation—experienced as they cared for a sick or dying loved one. But the goal of the group was to provide community beyond the social level and into the spiritual level. "There is a value and a power in checking in with people who are going through the same thing," Rabbi Fenner said. "But these women wanted to take it deeper. What does this mean to our lives, to our theology? These are the larger questions that are raised all the time, but have to be forced into the background by the immediacy of an illness."

At one evening meeting of the group, Rabbi Fenner led Phyllis and the three other women in an exercise derived from the Book of Lamentations, a portion of the Torah, which corresponds to what

Christians would know as the first five books of the Old Testament. Lamentations is a tale of woe, or misery and of complaint on a biblical scale. But on this evening, Rabbi Fenner turned its idea over to the women, handing them torn strips of paper and asking that they commit their own lamentations to print. Then, as the group sat in a circle lit only by candles, he pulled the strips one by one from a basket and read their lamentations aloud.

Phyllis's own feelings—of loss, of being worn and weary, of sometimes feeling like she couldn't go on—were "sanctified" in this way, she said; and she found this both freeing and moving. "I felt very enlightened to know that my problems were lamentations," she said. "To equate them with something from the Bible was very moving." Phyllis said she has never been very religious and only rarely attends temple. But as a result of her contact with the group, and especially her interaction with Rabbi Fenner, whom she describes as kind and gentle, she has found a renewed interest in her Jewish roots. This fall, she will take a course in the Jewish High Holidays at her temple, Rodef Sholom. Now, every morning as she prepares to swim laps before going to see her husband, she stands with her toes over the edge of the pool and prays, "Thank you, God, for bringing me to this moment."

Bringing Jews back into the synagogue is not one of the Jewish Healing Movement's goals. But, when it happens, "we are delighted for a number of reasons," said Rabbi Fenner. "A synagogue can be a place where people's Jewish communal connections can be a great sense of support and connection. To the extent that people feel more empowered to seek out sources they weren't seeking before, either in our tradition or in the synagogue, for us that is a wonderful outcome."

But why must the response to these questions be a Jewish response? What do the participants in Rabbi Fenner's group, and others originating from the movement, get that they could not get elsewhere? "There are multiple threads associated with this question," Rabbi Fenner said. "On a social level and on a deeper identity level, these women are all Jewish. Jewish life has been important to them. It has been their identity. Their Jewishness at some point represents the language of community. So it makes sense, as a place to turn. The Jewish community has an additional realm of support to offer and, in the sense that they felt isolation and distance and hurt, another level to heal."

"A sense of community is essential to understanding Jewish healing," said Rabbi Eric Weiss, executive director of the Bay Area Jewish Healing Center. "The entire Jewish faith is founded on community, relationships between Jews and between the Jewish people and God. On Mount Sinai, we agreed to covenant with God," he said. "We said 'yes' to God and God said 'yes' to us. We are a people. So our Jewish journey is communal. And," he continued, "Judaism has always contained the seeds of its own healing movement, though it has only recently come to nurture them as such. Within the traditional Jewish liturgy are prayers for the sick and the suffering, prayers for mourners, and prayers for health and strength. But, for whatever reasons, they have not been emphasized on their own. Maybe some of the spiritual aspects of Judaism have been subverted to the cultural aspects," Rabbi Weiss said. "We have kind of reclaimed that and made it part of this experience."

Another emphasis of the Jewish Healing Movement is the difference between "healing" and "curing." "Jewish life makes that distinction, and this is the crux of the movement," Rabbi Weiss said. "Someone can die of cancer because there is no cure, but they can die healed. It is possible to come to a state of reconciliation to one's state, to God, and to others. And Judaism holds that whatever happens to your body, your soul remains pure. So healing has to do with acknowledging the natural progression of one's physical life, coupled with the purity and immortality of one's soul." However, unlike the Christian tradition, there is little emphasis on an afterlife. "The notion of an afterlife is in Judaism," Rabbi Weiss said, "but it does not carry the same cultural weight as it does in other faiths."

While the basic thrust of the Jewish Healing Movement is to connect Jews with other Jews, with the Jewish community, and with God, it is also open to people of all faiths. Within Judaism, so far, it has been more widely embraced by the so-called liberal branches of Judaism—the Reform and Reconstructionist denominations. The aptly named Conservative movement has warmed to it, too; and the Orthodox and ultra-Orthodox, the more traditional of the Jewish denominations, have also turned to it, though somewhat less broadly.

Since its founding, the Bay Area Jewish Healing Center has become a kind of clearinghouse for information on how to establish healing programs around the country. But early on, its founders determined there was still a need for something more—something more religiously consecrated and sanctified than informal groups. In the early 1990s, Rabbi Nancy Flam, then the center's director, and Rabbi Yoel Kahn, leader of a predominantly gay and lesbian San Francisco synagogue, worked together to craft a liturgy for a healing service.

San Francisco was, perhaps, the perfect birthplace for a healing service. The Bay Area was in the teeth of the AIDS crisis, and Congregation Sha'ar Zahav, Rabbi Kahn's synagogue, had been hit hard. He had seen the need for some sort of healing service early on, and had been holding them regularly at the temple since 1988. The service was a collaborative effort, with different members of the congregation contributing poems, songs, and passages from Jewish texts. The result was a very personal, very intimate service; and it was held about once a month at the synagogue on Mission and Dolores Streets.

By the early 1990s, word of Sha'ar Zohav's service had spread, and inquiries from other congregations made their way to San Francisco. Rabbis and laypeople in other Jewish communities wanted to know how they could start their own Jewish healing services, suited to their own needs. In 1991, Rabbis Kahn and Flam decided to put the Sha'ar Zahav service into a more formal format. The result is *Shema Koleinu*, a liturgy for healing derived almost exclusively from Jewish sources.

Today, the Bay Area Jewish Healing Center holds three healing services a month, rotating between synagogues in San Francisco, San Mateo County to the south, and Marin County to the north. At a service held in Tiburon's Congregation Kol Shofar, Rabbi Weiss gathered four women from their community for a Thursday night healing service before the synagogue's ark, where its sacred Torah scrolls are housed.

On a small table at the front of the sanctuary were two small, white candles set in cut glass holders, a bowl of clear, cool water, and a small brown basket. The tender strains of a guitar filled the sanctuary as Marsha Attie, a singer and songwriter, strummed and sang a *niggun*, a wordless tune of prayer. The four people in the pews—all women apparently over forty—softly sang with her, "Lai, lai, lai, lai, lai." The music seemed to speak of pain and yearning. Everyone held a Xeroxed copy of *Shema Koleinu: A Liturgy For Healing*. As the song faded, Rabbi Weiss began the service by explaining the symbols on the table. "The water represents creativity," he said, and the basket was for the depositing of *tzedakah*, money that the center would donate to various charities.

Passing a hand over the candles, he said, "The candles are here to remind us that we live in a world that places a lot of emphasis on light. But we can't have a cycle of light without a cycle of dark. So these are here to commemorate both, because darkness can be both rejuvenating and positive. The Bible tells us we can't have new creation without a cycle of light and dark."

The service is twenty-six pages long and is written in Hebrew with both transliteration and an English translation. Over the course of the next ninety minutes, Rabbi Weiss picked through the service, skipping a page here and there, tailoring the service to what he deemed best. He asked the gathered if they would like to share what brought them to the temple tonight. One woman said she came to pray for a sick friend; another mentioned the strife in Israel. A third woman said she came for healing for herself and her husband. "I want to be like that bowl of water there," she said, "still and cool and peaceful."

Under the rabbi's guidance, the women thanked and praised God for the uniqueness of their souls, for the parts of their bodies that remained healthy, and asked for guidance as they navigated through their pain and loss. The service culminated in the group's recitation of the Sh'ma, a central prayer of almost all Jewish services:

Sh'ma yisrael Adonai Eloheinu Adonai Echad.
Baruch sheim kevod malchuto leolam vaed.
Listen, Israel, Adonai is our God, Adonai is One.

At the end, as a hush of peace and silence hung about the sanctuary, the women stood with Rabbi Weiss to chant the mourner's *kaddish*, a traditional Jewish prayer of remembrance. "May the source of peace send peace to all who mourn, and comfort to all who are bereaved. Amen."

Since formalizing this service in the mid-1990s, the Bay Area Jewish Healing Center estimates several hundred U.S. Jewish congregations have requested its use. All of them are free to adapt it as they see fit to meet the special needs of the sufferers within their own communities. The result is that these congregations have come up with something totally unique to their community of Jews. In Philadelphia, Rabbi Miriam Klotz established Miriam's Well, a healing center that routinely uses water as a symbol of renewal in its healing services. In Boston, Temple Israel's service has focused on the needs of caregivers from the eight hospitals that surround the temple. Susie Kessler, at the National Center for Jewish Healing, said there are probably as many different Jewish healing services as there are congregations that hold them. "They are a creative ritual, done outside of the regular mandated prayer periods," she said. "Because they are creative, they can be used to mark the end of a treatment, five years out of the woods [after an illness], or to commemorate a loss. They can be for congregations or for one person in particular. The goal is to unite people in prayer and silence and song, which are our spiritual tools. The Jewish Healing Movement is trying to reteach people the spiritual tools that are available in Judaism, many of which people don't think of as spiritual tools. It can be a little medicine chest. When times are tough we can find a box full of all kinds of stories from the Torah, from the Psalms, and they are stuff about every type of human emotion that exists."

Ruth Anne Faust is someone who took the idea of the Jewish healing service and expanded it into something special for her congregation, Bethel Temple, in West Hartford, Connecticut. She was moved to act after her mother died and she could find little within her knowledge of Judaism to draw on for spiritual sustenance. She discussed this seeming lack of resources with her rabbi, and, with help from the National Jewish Healing Center, she soon created Bethel Temple's first healing service. For the last five years, Ruth Anne Faust has facilitated monthly healing services at her synagogue, each based on a rotating theme, like grief, anger, despair, and suffering. "I try to make sure that each theme is broad enough that we can all connect to it," she said. "Coming together to honor these places of need is a very powerful experience, and we don't do that enough in our lives." She has recently begun adapting each service for distribution to other interested congregations.

At Bethel Temple, what Faust calls "the meat" of each service is a circle formed by the participants as they sing a song that asks God for healing. There are several pauses within the song, and during the silence she asks the gathered to consider the many things healing can encompass. "It is not always a physical cure," she said. "There are so many levels of living with ourselves and each other that can cause conflict." She recalled dying people who wanted to repair family relationships, or who needed to forgive themselves or others for their illness. "If we can find a way to let go of those things and the grief that comes with them, so much of our pain is diminished," she said. "It brings a level of healing that you just can't quantify."

Neo-Pentecostalism

Faith Healing and the Mainline Denominations

The "fire from heaven" of the 1906 Azusa Street revival, as Harvey Cox calls it in his book of the same name, spread rapidly across the United States and, eventually, to Europe, Asia and South America. This was the time when many Pentecostal denominations took root and spread—the Church of God, the Assemblies of God, and the Pentecostal Holiness Church among them. By and large, these churches drew their membership from working class people. American mainline Protestant denominations, generally a more middle- and upper-middle-class group of worshippers, and the Roman Catholic Church frowned on what they considered to be the antics of their Pentecostal neighbors— their talking in tongues, their raising of palms to the heavens, their falling to the floor, and their prediction of events, both dire and delightful. Many believed such signs and wonders and healing miracles died with the apostles in the first century.

But in the early 1960s, things began to change. America was undergoing a larger, cultural movement that affected everything from politics to religion. Americans, especially younger

Americans, turned away from the isolationism and complacency of the Truman and Eisenhower years, and gravitated towards the exotic and the experiential. This was the time when many spiritually hungry Americans left their familiar, homegrown churches and embraced the religions of the East. It was also a time when many Americans came to distrust formal organizations and began to clamor for power of their own. In religion, this led many people to abandon the hierarchical structures of the established, mainline churches in search of a more personal religious experience—a religious experience that they felt could somehow put them in more direct relationship with God. American mainline Protestant denominations saw the beginning of a long, slow decline in membership that has yet to revive. Catholics, too, began to watch a steady stream of their baptized brethren walk out the door. This yearning for the new, the experiential, and the mystical set the stage in the mainline churches for the entrance of divine healing and other miracles previously claimed almost exclusively by Pentecostals.

At the same time mainline membership was dwindling, the Pentecostal healing revival kicked off at Azusa Street was in decline. Some of the leaders of the revival had died, while others were struggling with charges of excess and poor management. Many Pentecostal churches expressed their disapproval of the healing revivalists by withdrawing their support of their ministries. Some of the more established and well-respected of these revivalists recognized the opportunity afforded them by the new and awakening spiritual hunger of the general populace, and focused their ministries more keenly on reaching non-Pentecostals.

One way the revivalists targeted their new audience was through the Full Gospel Business Men's Fellowship International, or FGBMFI. Started in the early 1950s, FGBMFI members generally had two things in common—a belief in the full gospel experience of speaking in tongues, healing, and prophecy, and a discomfort with old-line Pentecostalism. Founded in a small cafeteria in southern California, the group rapidly took hold and expanded, as original members recruited others, who then went on to found local chapters. Initially, the FGBMFI was addressed by a long list of old-time healing revivalists—Oral Roberts, Tommy Hicks, R.W. Culpepper, and O.L. Jaggers among them. But its growing respectability soon brought it to the attention of people who had never stepped inside a revivalist's tent. Several thousand people attended FGBMFI's first convention in 1954. One year later, the same convention was mainstream enough to attract Vice President Richard Nixon. Non-Pentecostal businessmen, drawn by the opportunities for fellowship and networking, soon began flocking to local chapters. By 1973, the FGBMFI had a membership list of 300,000 names and a budget of more than one million dollars. As David E. Harrell writes in his history of the healing revival, "Local chapter meetings in leading hotels put on display charismatic fervor in a dignified setting before a much broader and sophisticated audience than the revivalists ever reached."[1] Historian W.J. Hollenweger wrote that the FGBMFI "can claim credit for having gained a hearing for the healing evangelists in the non-Pentecostal churches."[2]

At the same time the FGBMFI was taking root, a number of old-time Pentecostal revivalists began reaching out to non-Pentecostals. Among the front ranks was Oral Roberts. In the 1960s, Roberts broke down denominational walls by holding ecumenical seminars on healing for ministers and laymen of all Christian persuasions at his eponymous university in Tulsa, Oklahoma. In 1968 he made a further move towards the mainline churches when he severed his ties to the Pentecostal Holiness

Church of his roots and officially aligned himself and his vast ministry with the United Methodist Church. The move shocked old-line Pentecostals, but, as Harrell writes, "Where most of Roberts' early supporters had been Pentecostals, his work came to depend heavily on sympathizers in the traditional churches. By the late 1960s, [Roberts] felt that his strongest backing came from the Methodist community."[3]

Television, too, brought healing evangelists like Roberts and Jimmy Swaggart into an ever-growing number of American living rooms. Beginning in 1969, Roberts aired a series of prime time television specials that reached 192 million people. A string of prominent, mainstream guests—from Billy Graham to Jerry Lewis—gave Roberts's healing ministry an even higher gloss of respectability. In an interview with Dick Cavett, Roberts explained that he hadn't abandoned faith healing, he had simply expanded the audience he was bringing it to. And when that audience returned to church on Sunday—be it a Catholic, Presbyterian, Lutheran or Methodist one—they brought their new exposure to divine healing with them. It wasn't long before a "trickle up" effect brought divine healing and other "gifts of the Spirit" into the mainline Protestant and Catholic churches, part of a new form of worship scholars have dubbed "neo-Pentecostalism."

The first outbreak of this new strain occurred in 1959, when Dennis J. Bennett, rector of St. Mark's Episcopal Church in Van Nuys, California, suddenly and unexpectedly began speaking in tongues. About 100 members of his congregation followed suit. This upset many other people in the parish, as well as the Episcopal bishop of Los Angeles. In the end, Rev. Bennett left the controversy in Van Nuys behind, but stayed within the Episcopal Church, moving to Seattle, Washington, where he took over the struggling St. Luke's parish. At the time of his arrival, St. Luke's had about two dozen members. Today, with thousands of members, it is a cornerstone of the Episcopal charismatic movement, which takes healing as one of its main foci.

On the Catholic side of the aisle, a charismatic revival burst on the scene in February 1967 at a small retreat weekend for students and professors at Duquesne University in Pittsburgh. In the middle of the retreat, students and professors alike began speaking in tongues, laughing uproariously, crying, raising hands to heaven in prayer and song—not the typical Catholic worship at that time. News of what came to be called the Duquesne Weekend spread, and within a short period of time there were charismatic gatherings in parishes across the country. By 1973, 35,000 charismatic Catholics gathered for worship at the University of Notre Dame. Today, there are 60 to 100 million Catholics worldwide who claim to have had some sort of charismatic gifts—speaking in tongues, miraculous healing, prophecy, and being "slain in the Spirit," or struck unconscious during worship. In the United States 250,000 out of 60 million Catholics are currently active in the movement; but 10 million, or one in six, have passed through it at some time.

At first, the mainline and Catholic versions of the gifts of the Spirit were more tame and watered down than that of their Pentecostal counterparts. Harvey Cox calls it a "milder and more domesticated version compared to actual Pentecostal services."[4] When these gifts did make their way into the traditional churches, they were almost always met with resistance. Some traditionalists were put off by what they thought of as its theatrics—the ecstatic nature of its tongues, testimonies, and prophecies. Then, in 1974, more than 1,000 people gathered in Washington, D.C.'s National Cathedral, an Episcopal church; and many of them broke out in tongues. One year later, 10,000 Catholics filed into St. Peter's Basilica in Rome. There, while Pope Paul VI looked on, many of them prayed in tongues. The charismatic gifts embraced by Pentecostals found a home in our nation's capital and in the seat of the Roman Catholic Church. It wasn't long before Methodist, Episcopalians, Presbyterians, and Lutherans began incorporating the gifts of the Spirit in their own churches.

The spiritually turbulent 1960s also gave rise to what have come to be known as the "new paradigm" churches; chief among them are Calvary Chapel, Vineyard Christian Fellowship, and Hope Chapel. Born on the West Coast, these churches were different, in that they were driven not by a denominational hierarchy or calendar, but by the experiences of their gifted pastors and their congregants. Gone was the emphasis on a pastor or priest in long, dark robes, who led quiet worshippers through rituals and teachings prescribed by their superiors and accompanied by the strains of a pipe organ. In their place came clergy in jeans and polo shirts who led enthusiastic people in music to the sound of electric guitars and synthesizers. A large part of this new experiential worship was healing.

The new paradigm churches have grown rapidly. Vineyard and Calvary each started with one congregation in the 1960s; but by 1996 they numbered 406 and 614 churches, respectively, in the United States. Calvary's initial church in Costa Mesa, California, has grown from two dozen members in the 1960s to more than 10,000 members today. Both Vineyard and Calvary are now officially large enough and organized enough to be called denominations, though they would shun the term; and each has more than 100 churches overseas. In this country, not a few of their new members are people who crossed the street from their traditional Episcopal, Methodist, Presbyterian, and Lutheran denominations. It wasn't long before clergy in those denominations began to take a look at what was driving folks into the new paradigm churches. When the mainline pastors saw the experiential nature of their neighbors' services, they tried to bring that into to their worship, too. Again, a new emphasis on healing was a part of what they brought.

Whatever the cause, almost every mainline Protestant denomination and Catholic diocese now has some formal healing movement under its organizational umbrella. The United Methodist Church has the Upper Room Healing and Wholeness Ministry, which has been training pastors in the spiritual dimension of physical healing since 1986. The Evangelical Lutheran Church in America oversees healing ministries through its various Lutheran Social Service agencies around the country; and though the Presbyterian Church in the U.S.A. has no official healing ministries, individual ministers and laypeople may organize healing services. In the Episcopal Church, the Episcopal Healing Ministry Foundation promotes the writings and teachings of Emily Gardiner Neal, a reporter-turned-deacon who helped draft and establish the church's official position on healing in 1964. There are also uncounted nondenominational and ecumenical Christian healing ministries, such as the Institute for Christian Ministries and the Institute for Christian Renewal.

But it is the Catholic Church that, with its 60 million members nationwide, is the largest Christian denomination to recognize faith, or divine, healing. Today, uncounted thousands of Catholics seek healing through pilgrimages, anointing with oil or holy water, intercessory prayer, and other rituals. Some of them, and some of their non-Catholic brethren, find their way to rural California, to one particular priest with healing hands.

Be Stouthearted and Wait for the Lord

The Story of Father Richard Bain

Look at his hands and they are nothing special—long, lean fingers that taper gently from supple knuckles to manicured nails. His hands bear no remarkable scars, no memorable lines, no distinguishing marks at all that would seal them in anyone's memory for very long. They are graceful hands for a man, and he moves them in delicate arcs when he gestures, as he often does when he speaks.

But thousands of people testify that there is, in fact, something very special about the pale hands of Father Richard Bain, a fifty-eight-year-old Roman Catholic priest at Sacred Heart Church in the tiny town of Olema, California. Tens of thousands of people seek him out each year to receive a touch from those hands, which they believe bestow God's healing upon them.

For fifteen years, Father Bain has traveled the country holding healing Masses and three-day parish missions. From his base in the Archdiocese of San Francisco, he has traveled from Vermont to Hawaii, Texas to Ohio. At his larger missions, a thousand people may show up, most of them in the hope that he can heal them or their loved ones of illness and disease. Many bring bottles, jars, and jugs full of water for the father to bless. They believe this holy water will cure them, their friends, and their loved ones, too, long after Father Bain has gone.

Over the years, Father Bain has collected dozens of letters from people who believe he has helped cure them of everything from acne to cancer. A woman from Las Vegas writes that Father Bain took away pain she had after surgery. Another woman from San Bruno, California, said her husband was healed of an arthritic knee. A nun in San Francisco describes how, after a blessing from Father Bain, a 70 percent blockage in her cardiac artery disappeared. And Joe Illuzzi of West Hempstead, New York, writes that he and his wife, who were planning to resort to in vitro fertilization, conceived a child the usual way after Father Bain laid his hands on Mr. Illuzzi.

And there is also Mary Ann Serrano, a fifty-nine-year-old homemaker who lives in Dillon Beach, California, just up the road from Olema. In 1998 she was diagnosed with esophageal cancer. After chemotherapy and radiation, her doctors gave her only two to four months to live. She could swallow nothing and just breathing was a misery. Then she went to see Father Bain. Now, three years later, she is cancer-free. "Statistically, it is impossible," she told me. "I had less than a one-in-a-hundred chance of survival. It is a definite faith healing. Definitely, the Lord healed me. There is no getting around that." Now, she volunteers at Father Bain's healing Masses, ushering the hopeful to the altar.

If Father Bain's hands look like nothing special, then it must be said that the rest of him follows suit. Meeting in his study at Olema's Sacred Heart Church, about an hour north of San Francisco, he looks more like Mr. Rogers than a priest. He wears a green cardigan sweater, a pinstriped shirt, and a pair of khaki-colored pants. On his feet are a pair of Birkenstock sandals—the

kind with two straps—and a pair of white socks. His hair is liber-
ally sprinkled with salt and pepper, as is his mustache. His voice
is comfortable, like his clothes, running smoothly up and down a
middle range. Walking up the stairs and down the hall, he takes
a rosary from his pocket and clicks the dark beads back and forth
between his hands.

When asked about his gift of healing, he explains it away. "I
don't think it is anything special," he says. "I think we all have this
power. I prayed for these people the way I was taught to, and I
really believe if anybody else did it, the same thing would happen."

Richard Bain was not always such a strong believer. Raised in
the Roman Catholic Church in San Francisco, he entered the
seminary at the age of nineteen. But he left after one year, feeling
the atmosphere was "too repressive." Some years after graduating
from the University of San Francisco, he stopped going to church
entirely.

After school, he started a career in business, working for a
San Francisco public utility. It was the early 1970s and the sexual
revolution was in high swing. The twenty-something Richard
Bain swung right along with it. Somewhere between the singles
bars and the discos, he let go of God. "That lifestyle is completely
contrary to the gospel," he says. "You can only live that lifestyle
for so long before you lose your faith, and that is what happened
to me." He went so far as to declare himself an atheist. "In my
own mind, I couldn't conceive of God. If I could conceive of a
God, he was very far away from me and didn't care about me."

So he threw himself into his work, rising very quickly to
become the youngest corporate officer at his public utility. Then
one day, a female coworker invited him to come with her to a
Bible study. A Catholic, she knew he had strayed from his faith
and hoped to get him to return. And, hey, he admits, she was

cute. "The reason I went was I was lonely," he says. "I didn't want to study the Bible. I just didn't have anything else to do that night."

Nothing monumental happened that night, but something took hold inside him. He remembers listening to the discussion and really enjoying it, and being surprised that he was enjoying it. After the meeting, he began thinking about God again. A couple of weeks later, while driving to Lake Tahoe "with a couple of girls," Richard Bain felt a very strong desire to go to confession. He and his friends stopped in Reno, and while they went to the casinos, he went to church.

But back in San Francisco, "I went back to my old ways," he says, going to bars, going home with women. Still, he continued attending the Bible study, and accompanied the group the night they decided to drop in on a gathering of charismatic Catholics at the old St. Ignatius High School, Bain's alma mater.

It was a revelation. Here were Catholic men and women—young, like himself—singing and dancing, swept up in the spirit of worship. There were guitars and tambourines, people raising their palms to God as they sang and prayed. And quite a few people spoke in tongues. There was an ecstasy in the worship that Bain had never experienced before. "There was just so much love," he says. "I felt something I had never felt before—the feeling of love, love of the Holy Spirit, and of God's presence."

The joy in the room instantly reawakened his faith and his desire to be back in the heart of the church. After the service, he waited in line to make his confession to one of the priests in charge. From that moment, he says, his promiscuity became a thing of the past.

Bain threw himself into the Catholic charismatic movement, attending its meetings every Saturday night. He signed up for an eight-week course on baptism in the Holy Spirit, an experience charismatics consider a necessary foundation for a close relationship with God. In the first class, on a Saturday night, the instructor told everyone their lives were about to change. It was something Bain took very seriously. It was what he had come there seeking. Two days later, he got a call from a friend in Hawaii, offering him a high-paying job as an executive with a construction company. Remembering the words of the teacher on Saturday night, he took the job on the spot.

Before he left for Hawaii, Bain wanted to complete the eight-week course. He was afraid if he left without completing it, the new-found fervor of his faith would disappear. So a woman from the class came to his apartment to guide him through the final steps.

The two stood in Bain's living room, his bay windows offering a view of San Francisco at night. She began to pray for him, asking God to grant him the spiritual gifts that come with baptism in the Holy Spirit—the gift of healing, among them. They prayed for a while, Bain remembers, but he felt nothing special. Then she began to speak in tongues and asked him to mimic her. He did, still feeling nothing. She then began to sing in tongues and he sang along with her. Still, he felt just as he had before. Finally, she said to him, "Richard, you have received the Holy Spirit."

"I asked her why she thought so because I didn't feel anything," he says. "And she said, 'Because you are singing in tongues.' And I said, no, I am not, I am just mimicking you. But something did happen because I was very peaceful about not feeling anything, and the old me would have been very disappointed. Then I said, 'Maggie, it is okay. I will receive the Holy Spirit when God wants me to.'"

At that instant, Bain recalls, a sudden gust of wind rushed by his window, rattling the glass. At the same time, he felt a rush run through him, from his head to his toes. "What I felt that night, it was unbelievable," he says. "It was just like in the Bible. I don't know if there were tongues of fire coming out of the top of my head, but I would not have been surprised if there were." He felt elated, drunk, and as high as he had ever been. He began talking, telling Maggie of what he felt coursing through him, and he noticed his words were slurred and that he was swaying from side to side. The effect lasted for days, and, he laughs now, his coworkers began talking behind his back about what a drunk he was.

With the rush of wind came a huge rush of faith. "After that, the sacraments came alive," he says. "The Bible became alive. I could sit and read the Bible for hours at a time. I found prayer very easy, too."

Once he got to Hawaii, settling in Honolulu, Bain found another charismatic group and dove in. They met every Friday night. And every morning at six A.M., he went to Mass. One morning, just after receiving Holy Communion and taking its wafer on his tongue, he had a thought: "I can become a priest." "I tried to put the thought out of my mind because I did not want to be a priest," he says. "I wanted some day to get married and have a family. Try as I might, I could not get it out of my mind. It just kept coming back."

It persisted long enough and strong enough that he applied to St. Patrick's Seminary in Menlo Park, California. Even there, though, he wasn't sure. "My first year in the seminary I remember walking alone on the grounds after dinner and thinking to myself, it's okay, I will quit at the end of the year," he says. "It was not until December of my second year that I finally got in touch with the call, and after that I really wanted to become a priest."

In 1977, in the middle of his second year at seminary, Father Bain attended a healing service held by the Rev. Francis MacNutt, a Catholic priest with a healing ministry of his own. At the service,

Father MacNutt taught how to pray for the healing of the sick. The key, MacNutt taught, is for the healer to pray that his hands become the hands of Jesus.

At the time, Father Bain was taking communion to eight shut-ins in St. Kevin's Parish in San Francisco. The next time he made his rounds, he asked each person if they had any condition or ailment they wanted him to pray about. Most had arthritis. Whatever they told him it was, Father Bain placed his hands on them and prayed as Father MacNutt had taught him—as though his hands were the hands of Christ. As soon as his next visit with them, some of the shut-ins told him they were better. Much better. Even so, Father Bain didn't see this as anything special. "I didn't see it as a gift," he continues. "I saw it as something Jesus was doing and not me. All I was doing was praying." Then, he adds, "because I had lost my faith and then got it back, I think I got it back differently. I was much more open and not so surprised by what God can do."

But the people who felt he helped heal them thought it was something special, and word of the new priest with the healing touch soon spread. In the summer of 1984, Father Bain invited Father Dennis Kelleher, a Catholic priest with a healing ministry based in New York City, to hold a healing Mass at his current assignment at Our Lady of Loretto Church in Novato, California. The two men talked and Father Kelleher encouraged Father Bain to start his own healing mission. The following January, he held his first Mass for healing in San Francisco, and by the following December he was invited to give a parish mission in Atlanta. With permission from the Archdiocese of San Francisco, Parish Missions, Father Bain's traveling healing ministry, was founded.

In the beginning, at Father Bain's healing Masses when he touched people on the head, many "went over," falling down in what is often called "resting in the Spirit" or being "slain in the

Spirit." Then, in 1987, about two years after starting the healing ministry, he read a book by Cardinal Joseph Suenens, in which the late cardinal warned that "the falling phenomenon," as he called it, had more to do with psychology and emotion than with a true spiritual experience. Cardinal Suenens concluded that "resting in the Spirit" is not a manifestation of the Holy Spirit and should therefore not be a part of the liturgy. It might also alienate those who did not experience it or were afraid of it. He advised all priests to discourage the practice.

At first, Father Bain resisted the advice. Then, out of respect for the cardinal, he decided to forego the practice. The change has only deepened his ministry, he says. "What I noticed was the Mass was more peaceful," he says. "I think it became much more contemplative. And I think it led people to find Jesus, not in something exterior, but in their own hearts."

Today, a Mass for healing with Father Bain is peaceful, almost somber. The overriding sense is one of reverence. Father Bain begins by telling the gathered that in the Mass they are about to celebrate together, they will experience "the most powerful form of prayer there is." First, a Parish Missions volunteer leads the gathered in saying the rosary. Over and over again, sometimes as many as a thousand voices repeat, "Hail Mary, full of grace, the Lord is with thee. Blessed art thou among women. Pray for us sinners now and at the hour of our death. . . . " It takes about a half hour to complete, and leaves a great hush in its wake.

At a healing Mass in San Francisco one foggy April night, about 300 people filled the tiny St. Brendan's Church in the Sunset District of the city. The surrounding neighborhood was upscale, nestled into a hill overlooking the rest of the city, but the people were from all different backgrounds. A woman in a beige pashmina sat in a pew near a man in torn and faded denim.

Several people came on crutches or with wheelchairs and walkers. Not a few had white hair.

After the rosary, Father Bain appeared from behind the altar. He told everyone that the Mass they were about to participate in "is the most powerful form of prayer, if said *right*. Right," he continued, "means together and with a full heart." Then a woman from the parish led the congregation in a psalm: "One thing I ask of the LORD; / this I seek: / To dwell in the LORD's house. . . . / Wait for the LORD, take courage; / be stouthearted, wait for the LORD!" (Psalm 27:4a,14 NAB).

For his homily, Father Bain took as his text the story of the loaves and fishes—how Jesus fed the gathered from only a few fish and the crusts of some bread. Then he said, "This reading says God does not ration the gifts of the Spirit. He gives everything fully. At these Masses, sometimes people say to me after [the Mass] I wanted my sister to be healed so I didn't ask him to heal me. So what does this mean? That God only has enough love to answer one prayer? The fact is you could write down a million prayers and to God it wouldn't make any difference. He doesn't ration, he doesn't ration the Holy Spirit. I believe God wants to give us more than we ask for. But sometimes we set limits and sometimes that determines what we are going to get. God wants to give us life in abundance. He wants to give us more than we expect."

Then, in preparation for the healings, he continued, "So when we come up today for the blessings, let's not come up for a little." Row by row, every person in the church arose, walked down the center aisle to the wooden communion railing, and waited with bowed heads for Father Bain to touch them. A woman began leading the congregation in the rosary, punctuated at times by the soft a cappella singing of the choir, also Parish

Missions volunteers. Moving from his left to his right, Father Bain walked along the opposite side of the railing, stopping at every two persons and placing one hand on each of them, crowning their bent heads with his palms. He paused only for four or five seconds before each pair, his lips sometimes moving silently, his eyes looking either down at their heads or across the church to a large stained glass image of Christ with hands outspread. He did not ask people what ailed them. "There is no need to," he explained later, "since it is coming from God." Over each person, he silently prayed the same prayer: "Come Holy Spirit, fill the hearts of thy faithful and kindle in them the fire of thy love. Send forth thy Spirit. They shall be recreated and thou shall renew the face of the earth." Then, he moved on to the next pair.

When a woman offered him a limp toddler in her arms, he bent to kiss the child's forehead. When another woman began to cry under his touch, his hand slipped momentarily from her head to her shoulder in comfort. After he passed by them, some people remained in prayer, others returned to their seats. All were silent.

About a week after the Mass, I visited Father Bain in his study, where an Orthodox icon of the Virgin Mary rests next to his computer. I wanted to ask him about the burden and responsibilities of being a healer. Why does he think God chose him for this work? How does he feel when someone he prays for does not improve, but perhaps dies? The questions seemed to perplex him.

"My responsibilities of being a healer," he says, "are all subject to my responsibilities as a priest, which include living a life that reflects God's love and God's goodness." Is that hard? "Not if you pray," he says. "If you have a deep, daily prayer life in which you are touched by the Spirit and you are being fed by that, it is very easy to live that life because you want to. That's not saying there aren't temptations. Padre Pio said there will always be temptations because God loves us. But if you have that deep prayer life, even with temptations, you will be at peace. You will be happy. It is only when your inner being isn't being fed by God that life becomes a struggle."

He never feels remorse when someone he prays for dies, because he knows that the healing comes from God, not from him. "All I can do is lay my hands on them," he says. "That is all I can do."

How does he answer, for himself and for the people he serves, why God heals some and not others? Why does God let bad things happen to people he supposedly loves?

"I really trust God," he says after a pause. "In all those hours of prayer, I have found that God is love. It is unbelievable how much he loves us." Then, after another long moment in which cars whish by on Highway One outside the window, he adds, "It is a mystery. But it is a mystery in the mind, not in the heart. Your mind is never going to figure this out. We are never going to get an answer that will satisfy us. But we can get a feeling. I have had people leave the Masses with a light inside of them, with a peace. They know their loved one is going to be okay, whether they recover or not."

As for his gift being a burden, he replies, "No more than it is a burden to have children you love, and I love it. I have come to see that this is what God wants me to do, and when God gives you a burden, it is light."

If Father Bain has a gift for healing other people, he does not have that same gift when it comes to himself. About ten years ago, he developed tinnitus, a chronic condition that produces a loud ringing in the ears. It is triggered by exposure to loud noises and only abates with quiet. Now, he must avoid large gatherings of people, can no longer attend or conduct weddings or funerals, go to the movies, parties, restaurants, or travel widely. It also keeps him from preaching the way he would like to. He can't raise his voice above the level of conversation, but must use a microphone. He can't have organ music at his services, only the soft singing of five or six unaccompanied voices. He must wear earplugs at every service he attends or officiates. At night, the ringing sometimes keeps him awake for long stretches. In 1998, he asked to leave St. Anselm's Church in Ross, California, where he was working full-time as director of the healing ministry in the Archdiocese of San Francisco, to become the pastor in Olema, a sleepy cluster of white clapboard buildings on the fringes of Point Reyes National Seashore. Now, outside his study window, he sees green leaves, blue sky, and brown cows.

Tinnitus can be caused when someone stands too close to a loud noise, like an exploding bomb, or by long exposure to a constant din, like the hum of factory machines. But neither Father Bain nor his doctors can trace the physical cause of his case. One day it was just there. But Father Bain has a theory. "If a healer has an ailment, he is going to be able to better identify with the people who come to be healed," he explains. "It probably also keeps him humble—so he knows he is not God. I look back on the fifteen years of suffering and I thank God for it. It was a real blessing. And I think God will take it away—when I become humble enough."

Humility doesn't seem to be a problem for Father Bain. There is absolutely nothing of the showman about him. He has no hunger for attention. At every Mass he tells people right from the beginning that they are here for God's miracles, not his. On his ministry's Website*, there is only one small picture of him. "I don't want people to discover Father Bain," he explains. "I want people to discover the church and Jesus and God's love."

---

*   www.parishmissions.com

Afterword

When I was in journalism school, one of my professors, Ari Goldman, a former religion reporter for the New York Times, told our class of sixteen "wanabees" that in order to win the Pulitzer Prize, we must truly experience the stories we wrote. If memory serves, he told us the tale of a rookie *Times* reporter assigned a story about a seemingly mundane topic, a new school lunch program. When the reporter turned in his story, he had all the details: why the school district needed a new lunch, how much it cost the taxpayers, what kind of nutrition it provided, and so forth. But he was missing the most critical part of the story, as his editor quickly pointed out; what did the lunch taste like? Was it good? Was it awful? And there, in the tones of that long ago *Times* editor, Professor Goldman pronounced the moral of the story: "You gotta eat the lunch."

Twice in the course of reporting this book, I decided to "eat the lunch." The first time was in St. Brendan's church, as I watched Father Richard Bain place his smooth hands on the bowed heads of the sick and the hopeful. Something inside me told me to put down my notebook, stand up, and take a place at the communion railing. I bent my head and closed my eyes in an effort not to anticipate his touch, but to experience it as honestly as my reporter's skepticism would allow.

While waiting for Father Bain to reach me, I tried to do as he had instructed the congregation and not hold back on what I would request of God. About a week before, I learned I was pregnant with my first baby. At 37 years old, I was at high risk of having a baby with birth defects or some congenital disease. So I asked God to please let me have a healthy baby.

Father Bain's hands were firm and gentle, and very warm. And the second they touched my head, I certainly felt something—a warm wave of energy that very swiftly passed from the top of my head to my toes. It surprised me. I didn't expect to feel anything. I am a religious person in the sense that I believe in God and I believe that Jesus Christ was a remarkable teacher who lived and died long ago, but I could not say that I believed in miracles. Yet I left the railing with a hand on my stomach, feeling that something had definitely passed between the priest and myself. I felt blessed. I felt reassured.

A month later, I had a miscarriage. My husband and I cried and held each other for a string of rough nights. But during the day, when he went to his office, I tried to go about my business as though nothing of import had happened. I got dressed, put on makeup, made phone calls, and tried to write this book.

But inside, I was devastated. Why me? I asked. Why us? What could I have done to deserve this? Was I being punished for some of the stupid things I did in my twenties? Was I unworthy of having a child? Was I too fat, too old, too selfish to have a baby? Why would God—who I felt had taken such good care of me until this point—want me to lose my baby?

Then, through the help of a friend, I came to see that, perhaps, God had given me what I asked for that day in St. Brendan's. I had asked God for a healthy baby. And one of the main reasons women miscarry, especially in the first trimester, is because the fetus is somehow unhealthy or unwhole.

Instantly, I felt a weight lifted from my shoulders. The miscarriage had not been my fault, nor was it a punishment for something I had done in the past. It was, I began to think, an act of God and realizing this left me feeling "healed." Did God heal me? In a sense, I think yes, though believing that requires that I redefine my idea of who God is and what he can, or cannot, do. Perhaps he is not, as I once thought, an all-powerful, all-knowing being who rewards us or punishes us at his will. Perhaps he is, I think now, an all-loving being who wants only the best for us, though we may not always understand what the best is.

I said there were two times when I "ate the lunch." The initial relief I felt at realizing the miscarriage wasn't something God would cause to happen to me lasted only a short while. Then the grieving process took over and I started to experience the symptoms of a broken heart: outbursts of anger, spates of crying, and an overall sense of the uselessness of my life. Each morning it was a struggle just to get out of bed. But each morning I did get out of bed and went about my day as if I were completely over it, as if things were just fine.

Then, about three weeks after my miscarrage, I attended a Jewish healing service in a round, wooden synagogue in Marin County. The service was not crowded—only three women were there with me, and the sanctuary was so hushed and peaceful with flickering candles and the strumming of a guitar, that again I felt compelled to participate instead of just watch. Under Rabbi Eric Weiss's direction, we came to the part in the service where we read aloud from a poem by an anonymous writer:

Tis a fearful thing to love what death can touch.
A fearful thing to love, hope, dream: to be—
To be,
And oh! To lose.
A thing for fools, this
And a holy thing,
A holy thing
To love.

At the end of the poem, I cried. Something had cracked inside my chest, and after the service I sat in my car in the parking lot for a while and cried some more. I cried for the baby I wouldn't have, and I cried for myself and my husband. Then I felt a lot better and drove home. Over time, the little hurt place in my chest where I carried the loss of the baby let loose and dissolved.

In "eating the lunch," I came to understand that to be able to believe in the healing power of God is to be able to love. To love another person, yourself, a child, a friend, even a pet. God is love and love is healing. And I learned that healing, whether you believe it is divine or otherwise, is ongoing. It seldom comes as a bolt from heaven, but blossoms inside the sufferer over time.

And what is God if not time? What is God if not patience? What is God if not eternal?

ENDNOTES

ONE

1. This was taken from a direct mail flyer sent to Mary Elizabeth Turk from Robert Tilton, which is now among Vicki Crenshaw's papers.

TWO

1. R.S.J. Barrett-Lennard, *Christian Healing After the New Testament: Some Approaches to Illness in the Second, Third, and Fourth Centuries* (Lanham, Maryland: University Press of America, 1994), p. 115.

2. James Randi, *The Faith Healers* (Amherst, New York: Prometheus Books, 1989), p. 19.

3. Stanley M. Burgess and Gary B. McGee, editors, Patrick H. Alexander, assistant editor, *Dictionary of Pentecostal and Charismatic Movements* (Minneapolis, Minnesota: Zondervan, 1988), p. 359.

4. Meredith McGuire, "Healing Rituals in the Suburbs," *Psychology Today*, January/February 1989.

FOUR

1. Leon Festinger, Henry W. Riecken, and Stanley Schacter, *When Prophecy Fails* (Minneapolis, Minnesota: University of Minnesota Press, 1956), p. 3—32.

2. Harold S. Kushner, *When Bad Things Happen to Good People* (New York: Avon Books, 1981), p. 134.

3. Festinger, p. 22.

FIVE

1. Harold G. Koenig, Michael E. McCullough, and David B. Larsen, *The Handbook of Religion and Health* (New York: Oxford University Press, 2001), p.47.

2. Ibid.

3. Ibid..

4. R. P. Sloan and others, "Should Physicians Prescribe Religious Activities?" *New England Journal of Medicine* 342 (2000): 1913-1916.

5. Harold G. Koenig, *The Healing Power of Faith: Science Explores Medicine's Last Great Frontier* (New York: Simon and Schuster, 1999), p. 27.

SIX

1. Caroline Fraser, *God's Perfect Child: Living and Dying in the Christian Science Church* (New York: Henry Holt and Company, 1999), p. 93.

EIGHT

1. Mark Larabee, "State Law Puts Children's Lives at Deadly Risk," *The Oregonian*, 22 April 1998.

T E N

1. David Edwin Harrell, Jr., *All Things are Possible: The Healing and Charismatic Revivals in Modern America* (Bloomington, Indiana: Indiana University Press, 1975), p. 148.

2. W. J. Hollenweger, *The Pentecostals* (Minneapolis, Minnesota: Augsburg Publishing House, 1972), p. 6–7. Quoted by David Edwin Harrell, Jr., *All Things are Possible*, p. 148.

3. Harrell, Jr., p. 152.

4. Harvey Cox, *Fire From Heaven: The Rise of Pentecostal Spirituality and the Reshaping of Religion in the 21st Century* (Reading, Massachusetts: Addison-Wesley, 1995) p. 106.

BIBLIOGRAPHY

ABC News's *PrimeTime Live*. Transcript #220, 21 November, 1991.

Archer, John. "PrimeTime Lies? ABC's Diane Sawyer and Three Televangelists Clash Over Who's Telling the Truth." *Charisma*, February 1992.

Balmer, Randall. *Blessed Assurance: A History of Evangelicalism in America.* Boston: Beacon Press, 1999.

——. *Mine Eyes Have Seen the Glory: A Journey into the Evangelical Subculture of America.* London: Oxford University Press, 1989.

Baradell, Scott. "Holy Deception? Callers turn to TV Phone Ministries for Help, but Critics Say They Are Often Deceived." *Dallas Times Herald*, March 10, 1991.

——. "The Mass Marketing of Bob Tilton." *Dallas Times Herald*, December 2, 1991.

——. "The Prophet of Prosperity: Televangelist Robert Tilton Wants to Pray for Your Miracle." *Dallas Times Herald*, June 24, 1990.

——. "Robert Tilton's Heart of Darkness: The TV Preacher Climbed to the Top By Stepping on Souls." *Dallas Observer*, February 6, 1992.

Barrett-Lennard, R.S.J. *Christian Healing After the New Testament: Some Approaches to Illness in the Second, Third and Fourth Centuries.* Lanham, Maryland: University Press of America, 1994.

Benson, Dr. Herbert. *Timeless Healing: The Power and Biology of Belief.* New York: Scribner, 1996.

Brenneman, Richard J. *Deadly Blessings: Faith Healing on Trial.* Amherst, New York: Prometheus Books, 1990.

Burgess, Stanley M. and Gary B. McGee, eds., Patrick H. Alexander, assistant ed., *Dictionary of Pentecostal and Charismatic Movements.* Minneapolis, Minnesota: Regency Reference Library, 1988.

Cohen, Debra Nussbaum. "Focus on Issues: Jews Taking New Approaches to Connect Faith and Healing." Jewish Telegraphic Agency, January 14, 1994.

——. "Jewish Spiritual Healing Moves into the Mainstream." Jewish Telegraphic Agency, November 17, 1995.

Cox, Harvey. *Fire From Heaven: The Rise of Pentecostal Spirituality and the Re-Shaping of Religion in the 21st Century.* Reading, Massachusetts: Addison-Wesley, 1995.

"Dallas Women File Lawsuits Against Tilton." [Abilene, Texas] *Reporter News,* April 4, 1992.

Decker, Twila. "Miracles, For a Price." *St. Petersburg Times,* August 9, 1998.

DesAutels, Peggy, Margaret P. Battin, and Larry May. *Praying For a Cure: When Medical and Religious Practices Conflict.* Lanham, Maryland: Rowman and Littlefield, 1999.

Doniger, Wendy, consulting ed. Merriam-Webster's *Encyclopedia of World Religions*. Springfield, Massachusetts: Merriam-Webster, 1999.

Eddy, Mary Baker. *Science and Health With Key to the Scriptures*. Boston: First Church of Christ Scientist, revised, 1994.

Felix, Cathy. "Saying a Mishaberah and Using the Power of Religion to Heal." *MetroWest Jewish News*, September 28, 1995.

Fernandez, Elizabeth. "Priest's Healing Hands Credited with Miracles." *San Francisco Examiner*, February 20, 2000.

Festinger, Leon, Henry W. Riecken, and Stanley Schacter. *When Prophecy Fails*, Minneapolis, Minnesota: University of Minnesota Press, 1956.

Flam, Nancy. "The Jewish Way of Healing." *Reform Judaism*, summer, 1994.

Fraser, Caroline. *God's Perfect Child: Living and Dying in the Christian Science Church*. New York: Henry Holt, 1999.

Harrell, David Edwin, Jr. *All Things Are Possible: The Healing and Charismatic Revivals in Modern America*. Bloomington, Indiana: Indiana University Press, 1975.

——. *Oral Roberts: An American Life*. Bloomington, Indiana: Indiana University Press, 1985.

Jones, Jim. "Two Dallas Women Sue Tilton, Allege Fraud, Emotional Pain." *Fort Worth Star-Telegram*, April 4, 1992.

Keefauver, Larry. *When God Doesn't Heal Now*. Nashville: Thomas Nelson, 2000.

Keeler, Bob. "Healing in the Temple." *Newsday*, May 7, 1996.

Kelsey, Morton T. *Healing and Christianity: In Ancient Thought and Modern Times*. New York: Harper and Row, 1973.

Koenig, Harold G. *The Healing Power of Faith: Science Explores Medicine's Last Great Frontier*. New York: Simon and Schuster, 1999.

Koenig, Harold G., Michael E. McCullough, and David B. Larson. *The Handbook of Religion and Health*. New York: Oxford University Press, 2001.

Kushner, Harold S. *When Bad Things Happen to Good People*. New York: Avon Books, 1981.

Kydd, Ronald A. N. *Healing Through the Centuries: Models for Understanding*. Peabody, Massachusetts: Hendrickson Publishers, 1998.

Levine, Art. "Detectives for Christ: Ole Anthony and his Merry Band Take on the Televangelists." *U.S. News and World Report*, December 8, 1997.

McAvoy, Tom. "Colorado Governor Signs Anti-Faith-Healing Bill into Law." *The Pueblo* [Colorado] *Chieftain*, April 17, 2001.

Miller, Donald E. *Reinventing American Protestantism: Christianity in the New Millennium*. Berkeley: University of California Press, 1997.

Miller, Ellen. "Parents in Faith Case in Court." *Denver Rocky Mountain News*, March 30, 2001.

Neal, Emily Gardiner. *The Reluctant Healer: One Woman's Journey of Faith*. Edited by Anne Cassel. Colorado Springs, Colorado: North Wind Books, 1992.

Randi, James. "Be Healed in the Name of God: An Expose of the Reverend W.V. Grant." *Free Inquiry*, spring 1986.

——. *The Faith Healers*. Amherst, New York: Prometheus Books, 1989.

Rodgers-Melnick, Ann. "Charismatics Celebrate the Spirit of the Movement." *Pittsburgh Post-Gazette*, June 25, 1997.

Sloan, R. P., E. Bagiella, and T. Powell. "Religion, Spirituality, and Medicine." *Lancet*, 1999.

Sloan, R.P., E. Bagiella, L. VandeCreek, M. Hover, C. Casalone, T.J. Hirsch, Y. Hasan, R. Kreger, P. Poulos. "Should Physicians Prescribe Religious Activities?" *New England Journal of Medicine* 342 (2000): 1913-1916.

St. Pierre, Nancy. "Fifth Widow Files Lawsuit against Tilton Ministry." *Dallas Morning News*, April 23, 1992.

——. "Two Dallas Women Sue Tilton, Allege Fraud." *Dallas Morning News*, April 4, 1992.

Talbott, Nathan A. "The Position of the Christian Science Church." *The New England Journal of Medicine*, December 29, 1983.

Weintraub, Simkha Y., ed. *Healing of Soul, Healing of Body: Spiritual Leaders Unfold the Strength and Solace in Psalms*. Woodstock, Vermont: Jewish Lights, 1994.

Welsome, Eileen. "Born to Believe: Church Members Had Faith That God Would Heal Their Children. But Often Faith Wasn't Enough." *Westword*, October 12, 2000.

"Where Are They Now: A Televangelist Update." *Christian Research Journal*, fall 1994.